Sylvanus Stall

How to pay Church Debts, and how to keep Churches out of Debt

Sylvanus Stall

How to pay Church Debts, and how to keep Churches out of Debt

ISBN/EAN: 9783743301252

Manufactured in Europe, USA, Canada, Australia, Japa

Cover: Foto ©ninafisch / pixelio.de

Manufactured and distributed by brebook publishing software
(www.brebook.com)

Sylvanus Stall

How to pay Church Debts, and how to keep Churches out of Debt

Sylvanus Stall

How to pay Church Debts, and how to keep Churches out of Debt

Price, $1.50, Net,

HOW TO PAY CHURCH DEBTS

.

AND

HOW TO KEEP CHURCHES OUT OF DEBT,

BY REV. SYLVANUS STALL, A. M.,

AUTHOR OF " PASTOR'S POCKET RECORD," " MINISTERS' HAND-
BOOK TO LUTHERAN HYMNS," ETC.

" Owe no man anything."—Rom. xiii : 8.

NEW YORK:
I. K. FUNK & CO., 10 AND 12 DEY STREET,
1881.

PREFACE.

This book is the outgrowth of an earnest desire to afford aid to the thousands of churches to-day burdened with debt, and to the thousands more which are struggling to meet current expenses. In these pages we have sought to show, not how we would do this work, but how the most successful pastors all over this country have done, and are doing it. We have had no pet theory to advocate, but have sought to bring to all who are entrusted with the financial management of churches such information and suggestion as would enable them to perfect a system already in use, or to substitute such a one as would help in advancing them in their return to the only perfect method—the ordained law of the tithe.

We have sought to present both the advantages and disadvantages which attach themselves to each system in a purely unbiased manner. Instead of arguing the case, we have briefly stated the arguments upon both sides, and left the reader, with a knowledge of his own situation, to select for himself.

SYLVANUS STALL.

ACKNOWLEDGMENT.

In response to an extensive correspondence upon the subjects treated of in this book, the author desires, for suggestive aid, to acknowledge his indebtedness to the following clergymen:

Rev. M. Rhodes, D. D.

Rev. Thomas K. Beecher.

Rev. Irving Magee, D. D.

Rev. W. F. Crofts.

Rev. Edward G. Thurber.

Rev. A. T. Pierson, D. D.

Rev. P. Felts, D. D.

Rev. C. A. Stork, D. D.

Rev. Henry H. Rice.

Rev. Nathan G. Parke.

Rev. S. C. Logan, D. D.

Rev. T. R. Smith, D. D.

Rev. H. A. Boardman, D.D.

Rev. E. R. Beadle, D. D.

Rev. W. P. Breed, D. D.

Rev. Stephen W. Dana, D.D.

Rev. William T. Beatty.

Rev. E. Bushnell, D. D.

Rev. David R. Frazier, D.D.

Rev. Loyal Young Hays.

Rev. George C. Yeisley.

Rev. J. H. Walter.

Rev. R. W. Clark, D. D.

Rev. George Reese.

TABLE OF CONTENTS.

CHAPTER I.

CHURCH DEBTS.

CHAPTER II.

HOW CHURCHES GET IN DEBT.

CHAPTER III.

HOW TO PAY CHURCH DEBTS.

CHAPTER IV.

HOW TO KEEP CHURCHES OUT OF DEBT.
(*ESTABLISHED CHURCHES.*)

CHAPTER V.

HOW TO KEEP CHURCHES OUT OF DEBT.

(NEW ENTERPRISES.)

CHAPTER VI.

HOW TO RAISE MONEY FOR MISSIONS, AND BENEVOLENT WORK.

CHAPTER VII.

THE SABBATH COLLECTION.

CHAPTER VIII.

THE TITHE, FREE-WILL OFFERING AND ALMS-GIVING.

HOW TO PAY CHURCH DEBTS,

AND

HOW TO KEEP CHURCHES OUT OF DEBT.

CHAPTER I.

CHURCH DEBTS.

HINDER THE GOSPEL—SHOULD RETURN TO GOD'S METHOD
—NOT OF HEATHEN ORIGIN—NOT SANCTIONED IN THE
BIBLE—THE PARALYZING EFFECT—"ATTRACTING OUT-
SIDERS" A DELUSION—THE GREATEST SUFFERERS IN
THE CHURCH-DEBT POLICY—DEFEAT CHRIST'S DESIGN
IN ESTABLISHING THE CHURCH—THE CHURCH IN BOND-
AGE TO THE WORLD—DESTROY CONFIDENCE IN THE
CHURCH—FATAL TO EVERY BENEVOLENT ENTERPRISE
—SHOULD NOT DEDICATE CHURCHES IN DEBT—FOLLY
OF PRETENDING TO DEDICATE WHAT WE DO NOT OWN
—A NEW DEDICATORIAL SERVICE SUGGESTED.

Church debts are more than grievous burdens.
They are great hindrances to the spread of the gospel
and the salvation of men. They aid Satan to retain
his usurped possession of the world; and, during the
half century past, he has been using this subtle and
deceptive scheme with great success. The church has
fallen into the hands of the despoiler, and the present
condition of the Christian church demands a change

2

of financial policy—not a *new*, but a return to the OLD and God-given method. When Moses was about to erect the Tabernacle he appeared before the people with these words : " This is the thing which the Lord commanded, saying, Take ye from among you an offering unto the Lord: whosoever is of a willing heart, let him bring it, an offering of the Lord ; gold, and silver, and brass."

Church debts are nowhere sanctioned in the Bible, either by precept or example. Neither does the custom of loading churches with debt come from the heathen. The temples of the Hindoos, the Mosques and Musjeeds of the Mohammedans, the temples and " towers of silence " of the followers of Zoroaster, the sacred caves of the Buddhists—each and all structures set apart for religious purposes by heathen nations are dedicated and remain free of debt.

Not in the Bible, either among the ancient Jews or in the Primitive church, do we find anything of this destructive church-debt policy. But in Christian America expensive and debt-burdened churches are to be found everywhere. Their numbers overstep the boundaries of hundreds, and press into the thousands. The proportion is not diminished, but rather increased. The situation is one which demands the earnest thought and hearty co-operation of all Christian people.

A church debt has very justly been denounced as

"a church curse." It paralyzes every energy of a congregation. The grand possibilities of hundreds of congregations are to-day lost, both to the church and the world, simply because financial perplexities crowd out nobler thoughts, and leave no room for spiritual and eternal things.

The theory that a new church and a popular minister will attract outsiders, increase the membership and pay the debt, is a dangerous delusion. The principle is untrue, both in the business of the world and the affairs of the church. People will pay with some cheerfulness toward the success of a new enterprise, but when solicited to contribute toward an undertaking already so unsuccessful as to be embarrassed with debt, they will give sparingly as well as grudgingly, for in church affairs as in every thing else, "nothing succeeds like success." If a church, therefore, would be prosperous and useful it must shun everything which looks like church debt, whether great or small.

Instead of aiding to increase the membership, a new church, struggling under a heavy debt, or perhaps mortgaged for more than it would bring under the hammer, invariably repels the very class it was designed to attract and capture. Men who are not personally responsible for a debt, which they had not the pleasure of aiding to contract, are very slow voluntarily to assume it. New comers, and old residents, when seeking a spiritual home, will search out those free from encumbrance, and avoid most studiously every church with a debt. In this way the debt saps the best interests of the church, causing it to waste away because of unreplenished life.

The greatest sufferers in this ruinous church-debt policy are not usually among the laity, but among the clergy. Too often congregations " bind heavy burdens and grievous to be borne," and lay them on the minister's shoulders ; but they themselves will not move them with one of their fingers. The crushing responsibilities, or undue anxieties, are left to exhaust his physical energies, to make unlimited demands upon his mental activities, and to unfit him for the duties both of the pastoral and ministerial office. To be efficient in his calling, these matters should be entrusted to persons properly appointed to that department of church work. The apostles, that they might give themselves entirely to the ministry of the word, intrusted these auxiliary matters into the hands of those competent to superintend them. It was " not reason that they should leave the word of God to serve tables," neither is it reasonable nor right that ministers should now leave the word of God to be slaves to a church debt.

If a minister is left to struggle with desperate financial difficulties all the week, there can be in his

Sabbath ministrations but few "thoughts that breathe and words that burn." But the fact that the church has a debt is given as a conclusive reason why his sermons, clear, logical and convincing, should be clothed in choicest language, beautifully adorned with illustrations winnowed from history, science and the harvested literature of the ages. He must "draw" and pay the debt, or give place to one who will. Excellent pastoral qualities, spiritual graces, intellect and learning, all these pass for naught. Debt begets a feverish thirst for sparkling and sensational preaching. The servant of God who seeks the perfecting of the saints, the edifying of the body of Christ, and the imparting of "the light of the knowledge of the glory of God," is passed by for one who will cater to every taste, and regard the wishes of men rather than the commands of God. Next to the necessity which compels hundreds to eke out a respectable living on an insufficient salary, church debts are despoiling the gospel ministry of most of its efficiency and usefulness.

They also serve to defeat the design which Christ had in establishing the church. The edifice should be erected and dedicated to the worship of Jehovah, the preaching of the gospel and the salvation of souls. Instead of these, how many churches are sacred only to the purpose of attracting men of means who shall help to pay for the unholy trap in which they have been caught. " The foolishness of God is wiser than men." God " hath chosen the foolish things of the world to confound the wise ; and God hath chosen the weak things of the world to confound the things which are mighty ; and the base things of the world, and the things which are despised, hath God chosen." But the church in debt feels that prudence (!) demands another policy, and so the worldly rich are gathered, both small and great, into the church. These men are counseled, placed in positions of trust, elected to office, and how often are men of wealth or influence in the world, and without religion, allowed to determine the question and say who is to feed the flock of Christ ? Their opinions are preferred to that of the children of God, simply to secure their aid in supporting the man of their choosing. How many pulpits are to-day spiked by the devil in this very way ? " Know ye not that the friendship of the world is enmity with God ? whosoever therefore will be a friend of the world is the enemy of God." The voice from Heaven says : " I will make a common man more precious than fine gold, and a great man than the golden wedge of Ophir." Why then seek the rich, rather than the poor ? Why convert the house of God into a house of merchandise, or forfeit the freedom of God's people by selling the house of God in slavery to sin ? The borrower is *always* the slave of the lender.

Another and very sad result of church indebtedness is the great distrust which it begets in a community. Claims presented remain unpaid and the church falls into disrepute. Persons untaught in these matters, naturally expect—and have a right to expect from the principles taught in the Christian church—that claims against its organization would be most promptly met when payment is demanded. When, however, one after another becomes wearied of pressing claims that remain unpaid, the church is spoken against, and as a result these persons are largely lost to the power of the truth. The influence does not stop here, but the injudicious, if not dishonest, policy is denounced by all fair-thinking people, and may proceed so far as to close to the church every avenue of usefulness in a community. It is but fair to expect the church to maintain and practice those principles which it was established to teach.

Another result of this unsound policy is its inevitable tendency to extinguish every benevolent sentiment of a congregation. It allows selfishness to flourish in great luxuriance, while the church debt is made the apology for turning a deaf ear to every appeal for aid. The beneficence of the church decreases, until in Christian giving the congregation becomes virtually a cipher. These congregations often appear most patriotic upon the parade ground, but in the great contest for the right, they are cowardly poltroons, living under a government which they will neither support nor defend. If the cause of home and foreign missions, the various benevolent operations of the church at large and the poor at home were merely left to care for themselves while an honest effort was really made to liquidate the church debt, there would be some apparent weight to the worthless excuse. But the apology is a mere pretext; they neither aid others, nor pay the debt. Congregations struggling honestly with burdensome indebtednesses are truly worthy of our sympathy and aid. It is rare, however, that con- gregations willing to pay their bills are found in debt. The debt-burdened congregations are usually of those which desire to do all the building and have the " out- siders " do all the paying. Now the " outsiders " are supporting the many institutions dependent upon them, at an expense fifty-fold greater than it costs to sustain the church, and it is sheer injustice to leave them to do all the paying while the church stands idly by. The church is to give to save the world, and not the world to save the church. Let us not re- verse the order, or lose sight of the specific purpose of the church. Her only work is to labor for the salvation of men, and no work in which she can engage, not even the building or paying for church edifices, can ever, in any degree, compensate for the neglect of this duty. The Savior's last command is: "Go ye into all the world, and preach the gospel to every creature," and we *must* obey it.

A change in regard to dedicating churches before they are paid for would tend largely to correct this disastrous condition of affairs. Let ecclesiastical bodies set themselves right in the eyes of the world, and correct this great evil among the churches, by refusing to formally dedicate any and all churches not fully paid for. It is commendable for congregations to build costly churches when they can pay for them without hindering their mission work, and the people who continually murmur because of the money lavished on temples built for the worship of God, would also have murmured, had they been with Jesus, because the alabaster box of ointment "very precious" was not sold for much and given to the poor; so let their murmurs be weighed against their worth. But let the united voice of the church go up against this great evil.

Congregations which are injudicious and visionary in their church plans, are wont to regard their cherished purposes all consummated when the church is dedicated. Whether it is paid for or not seems foreign to their minds. The question is simply one of whether mason, carpenter, painter and frescoer have completed their work. Whether the congregation have accomplished their duty does not enter into the consideration. Whether God will be pleased with the unpaid-for offering is not asked. If it is not an acceptable offering, selfishness, personal pride and sectarian vanity must be gratified, and so, " ministers of God, old and young, the elders and the people, all assemble. A sermon is preached, the liberality (!) of the people is commended, the beauty of the house is praised, great castles are built about prospective good, and perhaps that very house, it is predicted, will be a grand means of hastening on the millennial day; songs of praises are sung, God's name is invoked, and the house is most solemnly given to God," and one man at least, " rejoices with trembling "—he is the man who holds the mortgage ! Is it not absolutely ridiculous for any person, or persons, to set apart, dedicate or consecrate to the worship of God that which they do not own ? The principle which makes cheating or stealing dishonest is, that we seek to enrich ourselves at the expense of others, and God will not accept at the hands of any that which is made the means of defrauding and impoverishing another. If a number of persons with misguided zeal were to gather about a private residence, not their own, and by imposing ceremonies offer it to God, setting it apart for sacred purposes, no one would for a moment suppose that God would accept the gift or bless the givers. The thought of an organization of enlightened, intelligent people, with public parade and imposing ceremonies, setting apart to the worship of God a building which they have not paid for, and do not own, strikes the ordinary mind as ridiculous, if not sacrilegious or profane. To those who *will* persist in this irreligious, or wicked course, we would recommend that to the .other sins they no longer add that of attempting to deceive God. Be frank. Tell God and the community just how the matter stands, and upon what conditions it is given. Such congregations will need a new formula of dedication, and for their use we might suggest the following, recommended by Dr. J. G. Holland, and which may be slightly changed to suit the circumstances : " We dedicate this edifice to Thee, our Lord and Master ; we give it to Thee and Thy cause and kingdom, subject to a mortgage of one hundred and fifty thousand dollars ($150,000). We bequeath it to our children and our children's children, as the greatest boon we can confer on them (subject to the mortgage aforesaid), and we trust that they will have the grace and the money to pay the interest and lift the mortgage. Preserve it from fire and foreclosure, we pray Thee, and make it abundantly useful to Thyself—subject, of course, to the aforesaid mortgage."

CHAPTER II.

HOW CHURCHES GET IN DEBT.

INJUDICIOUS EXPENDITURES OF CHURCH OFFICERS—UN-
GUARDED ACTION OF COLLECTIVE BODIES—ACCUMULA-
TION OF SMALL DEBTS—UNDUE EXTRAVAGANCE IN
ERECTING SOME CHURCHES—INEFFICIENT BUILDING
COMMITTEE—ADOPTING AND AFTERWARD CHANGING
AN IMPERFECT PLAN—UNDUE HASTE IN ERECTING
CHURCHES—WANT OF JUDICIOUS PERSONAL SUPERVIS-
ION—DISINTERESTEDNESS AND PARSIMONY OF AN EN-
TIRE COMMUNITY—REMEDIES SUGGESTED—FREQUENT
CHANGE OF PASTORS—UNPAID SUBSCRIPTIONS—RESTING
THE ENTIRE CHURCH UPON ONE INDIVIDUAL—SEVERAL
UNSCRIPTURAL MOTIVES CONSIDERED—SUNDRY OTHER
WAYS ENUMERATED—CONCLUSION.

There are *many* ways by which churches get in
debt. Some of the more common may, we trust, be
considered with profit. Let us, then, traverse the
field and mark the places of danger, that others passing the same way may take warning lest they fall into
the same mistakes and come to the same sad end.

I. One class of churches becomes involved in debt
on account of the injudicious expenditures of the
church officers, or financial agents of the church.

When the financial interests of a church are committed to the control of chosen men, it becomes their

duty to inform themselves as to the financial ability of the congregation, and, in all cases, this is to be the bounds, beyond which they may not pass. They are entrusted with the duty of judiciously applying the means really at hand, and not under any consideration to invest the *anticipated* resources of the church — resources which should be expended no sooner than a prudent laborer would invest his money before he has earned it, and consequently not his at all. Not only is it unbusiness-like, but when prompted by improper motives it becomes disgraceful and even dishonest, and especially is this so when the income is not to fall due during their tenure of office. They apply that which is not theirs to apply, and leave their successors to struggle with difficulties and debts previously created, and by them inherited. The financial wardens of the church, being often unduly in a hurry, worried and burdened with their own affairs, and becoming neglectful of the best interests of the church, purchases are often made when the treasury will not warrant. These become very poor investments for the church, simply because sufficient time was not allowed for the selection, nor due regard given to the price. In short, men who are business-like and judicious in the transaction of their own affairs, often become very injudicious and unbusiness-like in the transaction of the affairs of the church.

II. But perhaps a more frequent cause of church indebtedness arises from an entirely different source.

To secure harmony of action it is sometimes rendered necessary to call a church, or congregational meeting to consider the propriety of certain courses of action. In these, as in all public assemblages, there are usually those who will volunteer to do all the talking and none of the thinking, and the result too frequently is, that promiscuous gatherings are led to vote burdens upon the financial guardians of the church, and then go home never to give the matter any pecuniary aid, or wise council. In almost all cases where such assemblages are called, it should be simply to take action upon plans previously wrought out by careful deliberation and continuous study. It is said, " to invent begin to think, and then keep on thinking." Thinking must precede talking, or if the congregation at large is left to invent plans, and devise ways and means, the greater probabilities are that their half-fledged ideas, when put to the test, if they should flap and flutter about for a time, will finally come to the ground in embarrassing confusion.

The custom of laying every matter of minor import before the congregation is fraught with much danger. When matters of great importance are to be acted upon, it will often serve as an excellent means of awakening, in the minds of the people, an interest upon the subject, and help them to place confidence in measures which they are permitted fully to understand, and for the carrying into effect of which they are expected to contribute of their means, or lend their aid. In order to succeed in some congregations, such a course is absolutely necessary, for some men of prudence and sagacity must understand a project thoroughly or they will not give it their aid. This is right and proper. But it is dangerous and detrimental to any church to submit to the congregation every matter of trifling moment. It simply affords an op-portunity for diversities of opinion, which finally be-get factions, and dismember congregations, for some men will never recant when once publicly they have expressed, or advocated an opinion. It is well to take wise counsel, but no general assembles his soldiers to give advice at a council of war, for it would only be productive of diversity and confusion. If the church officers are elected for anything, it is to act and bear the responsibility in all minor matters. If the con-gregation has no respect for their opinion, or confi-dence in their judgment, they should not have elected them to these responsibilities, or if done unadvisedly, the error had better be corrected by allowing such officers to give place to others better qualified; for, in church, as in state, some one must be entrusted with the responsibility of leadership. A poor general is better than none at all, at least when the choice lies between these two evils.

III. Another way by which churches become embarrassed with large debts, is by the accumulation of smaller and more trifling ones.

Under no circumstances should a congregation allow these small arrearages to accumulate, and despoil the church of its honor and usefulness. Never let a church live beyond its income. Yet it should not be forgotten that some people are ever harping on the one string of cutting down expenses, while they only prove their motive to be penurious and selfish, by being unfavorable, and even hostile, to any and every reasonable attempt to increase the income of the church to meet its pressing needs. Some men spend more time, and die meaner, trying to get their wants down to suit their income, than others do trying to get their income up to meet their wants. Every church should do as much as is in its power, but not outrun its ability to close up all accounts at the end of each year.

There are many successful and prosperous churches, which owe much of their usefulness to the fact that they allow no arrearages from year to year. In some churches, however, where this policy is pursued they fall into an error almost equally fatal. In all the various denominations, there are a few churches which permit, or cause this burden of furnishing the money

4

needed for the annual settlements, to fall upon the wardens, or officers. The result of this course is evident. This financial burden, oft repeated, and superadded to a disinterested spirit upon the part of the congregation, finally becomes so grievously heavy, that judicious and competent officers, taxed and censured beyond endurance, eventually retire to let the interests of the church fall into the hands of others less competent. It is a process by which many congregations accomplish the old addage of " riding a free horse to death."

The policy of another class of over-prudent officers is to assume the unprovided-for debts, without submitting them to the congregation for payment. This course, although slower, accomplishes the disastrous result nevertheless surely. The congregation grows into an indifference concerning the affairs of the church, caring little or nothing whether the amounts paid annually by the officers be much or little. Gradually the benevolence of the individual members becomes so dwarfed by the injudicious liberality of the officers, that when death, removal, or loss of property throws the church upon the resources of its members, it at once becomes evident that the congregation has lost the grace of giving. Officers should give to the support of the church, but should not be allowed to do all the giving, any more than all the praying, singing, or other worship.

IV. Another class of church debts find their origin in the undue and unnecessary extravagance displayed in the erection of some churches.

What we mean by extravagance, is that expenditure, which, whether necessary or unnecessary, creates obligations beyond the possibility of the congregation to pay. What is extravagance to one congregation may be parsimony and meanness for another; and likewise that undue withholding from the Lord which renders some congregations parsimonious and mean, would entitle others to respect for their economy and prudence. We are not in sympathy with those who are unwilling to render to God the richest treasures of architecture and beauty; the treasures of the nation were made tributary to the building of a temple where should dwell the radient presence of Jehovah. Forty-eight thousand tons of gold and silver, with sparkling gems and jeweled stones, wrought and polished by men of greatest skill, were required in the construction of the building of which God was the architect.

A cheap church in a rich community is an open and public proof of the poverty of religious sentiment and Christian life. In beauty, cost, and comfort, God's house should be superior in each community to the dwellings of men. God demanded that the offerings made to him should be without spot and without

blemish—they were to be the *best.* The richest and
most costly church that any congregation can build,
without incurring debt, will tend to beget charity
and foster piety, rather than to stimulate vanity and
pride. There are those always deprecating any considerable expenditure in church building, who plead
the necessities of the poor and the requirements of
missions; and it is only to be regetted that while
these persons contribute but little for churches, they
give less for either home or foreign missions. The
feeling which they feign is a mere pretext—an excuse
for not giving.

But while all churches should be models of beauty
and richness in the communities in which they are
located, they should yet not be so far in advance, as
to render the cost beyond the ability of the congregation to pay. A church edifice is simply a means to an
end, and that end is the salvation of souls, and the
saving of men. Where this object is lost sight of,
the church edifice may be, and often is, made a great
impediment to spiritual growth and religious life.
When the minds of the pastor and the church officials
are perplexed and burdened with financial embarrass-
ments, and their best energies exhausted to meet accruing obligations, but little strength is left for the
performance of other duties which are the heart and
spirit of the Christian church. Many a minister be-

comes a mere financial agent, being despoiled of usefulness because of perplexing church debts, entailed
upon him and his successors by some visionary enthu-
siasts.

V. Some church debts find their origin in the fact
that often those whose occupation and experience
qualify them to act on the building committee, plead
the pressure of business, and are unwilling to assume
the responsibilities of the position. As a result, the
work is committed into the hands of those less competent, and not infrequently is the minister, already
overburdened with the labors of his pulpit and the
duties of his pastorate, compelled to accept the burden, or consent to see the project fail. He is compelled
to serve until the work is complete, and then almost
universally to be pressed into service as a scape-goat
for the sins of the committee, or the congregation,
while another is called to stand in the temple he has
erected.

Now, we would not say one word against those
whom, as a class, we regard as among the most schol-
arly, self-sacrificing and devout in our land. Nor do
we speak but to their praise, when we say, that the very
character of their calling and study tends to make
them less proficient as business men. True, the ministry can produce some men as competent to supervise
vast enterprises, and control large interests, as are to

be found in any other of the walks of life. These,
however, are of those who possess a natural business turn, or have received a thorough business
education before entering the ministry. To their
abilities as preachers, they unite the desirable qualifi-
cations of good financiers and excellent managers.
There are some such in the ministry, but they are not
in the majority. Most ministers are altogether without any considerable experience in commercial life,
and for want of that knowledge which comes from
practice and experience, would be but poorly qualified
to engage in any financial or commercial enterprise for
themselves, and, as a matter of course, are but poorly
qualified to superintend similar interests for a congregation, composed of men skilled in the various departments of trade and commerce.

However desirable it might be to make a committee-
man of the minister, because of his knowledge of the
requirements of a church building, its acoustic pro-
protions, architecture, etc.—of his fund of learning,
and knowledge of other church edifices, and of his
interested, and perhaps more unbiased judgment than
any other man in the congregation, yet he can only
occasionally be selected on account of his business
tact, or financial ability. Most ministers will render
more useful and efficient service as a balance wheel to
the committee, rather than as a driving wheel for the
congregation.

The men entrusted with the superintendence of a new enterprise should be of those who, of all the congregation, are best qualified by knowledge and experience, and for no personal consderations, either of business or pleasure, should they regard it possible for them to escape the reasonable and moral obligations they are under to accept the responsibilities of the position. If they have talents fitting them for the work, God will demand why these talents have not been exercised, as well in the church as in the world. Ordinarily a church will last for more than a generation, and but few men are ever upon a building committee a second time. Each committee enters upon a work with which they are entirely unacquainted. While judicious, and perhaps men well chosen, they may never before have erected a building of any kind, and concerning the character and cost of material needed in constructing a church, know almost absolutely nothing, because their attention has never been called to that subject. If they were called upon to build a second church, after the experience they have had in building the first, they would be able to do it both better and cheaper.

It is most necessary, therefore, for each committee to avail themselves of the experience of others. Churches similar in size and construction to the one to be erected should be examined, and useful lessons learned from the excellencies and defects of others. Inefficiency or incompetency in the committee is without excuse, so long as any source of information remains unexplored and unimproved.

VI. Not unfrequently do congregations involve themselves in unnecessary debt by hastily accepting a plan or draft for a church edifice which has no adaptation to their wants and necessities. The work is begun, and when the immature ideas take shape in brick and mortar, it is found necessary continually to modify the plan and make alterations in the construction of the building. These changes, if made before the final adoption of the plan, would be attended with no expense, but when made after the work is begun, they are attended with unnecessary expense to the congregation, injury to the proportions of the edifice and the durability of the structure. Such changes, always expensive, should be guarded against with the greatest care. Such a defective plan is illustrated in the Grand Central Depot, in New York City. All the departing trains start on the western track, and have to cross the tracks of the arriving trains to get on the eastern track, that they may " keep to the right, as the law directs." So, also, must all arriving trains cross the track of the departing trains, in order to reach that part of the depot which by mistake the architect placed on the wrong side of the building. The sides of that grand building should have been reversed. A somewhat similar mistake in the plan was discovered too late for alteration, in a depot in Cincinnati, Ohio. Similar illustrations are found in churches.

VII. The cause of the indebtedness of many churches may be traced to a national characteristic of the American people. We are a nation of hurriers. Our haste would be becoming to those having the whole world before them, rather than to those most westward in the course of empire. The pulse beats quick, and as a nation we are at fever heat. We walk fast, talk fast, eat fast, act fast, borrow much, and get in debt fast. When we build a church, the work must be carried forward like every thing else—in a hurry. Instead of awaiting those seasons of the year when the price of material is lowest, and labor cheapest, frequently with but little regard to the expense, the work is hurried to completion. We too often begin with the unfounded assumption that necessity requires the edifice to be completed by a fixed day, not far distant, and if the money is not at hand, the best interests of the church are sacrificed to attain this end. The church is built not only faster than it can be paid for, but with an extravagance both unwarranted and unnecessary.

Why be in unnecessary and expensive haste? Solomon's Temple was seven and a half years in building.

5

The cathedral of St. Peter's, at Rome, was one hundred and seventy-five years in building ; that is, from the laying of the foundation to the date of dedication. If we include the work done under Pius VI, then three and a half centuries passed away, during which time 43 Popes reigned and died. The cathedral at Milan was begun in 1386, and was not completed until a grand impulse was given to the work during the conquests of Napoleon I. St. Paul's, in London, was only thirty-six years in building. The noted Cologne Cathedral was begun in 1248. The work in the interior is incomplete, and the scaffolding for the erection of the tower is but little higher than the ridge of the immense roof. Although of more than ordinary proportions, these buildings could readily have been completed in a much less period. It was not for want of men or material. With the exception of the first, it was for want of money to complete without the creation of immense indebtedness. Progress and finances kept step.

The plan of building and paying for a chapel, and then, as circumstances permit and necessity requires, beginning the work upon the church edifice proper, and carrying the work forward gradually and prudently, proves both satisfactory and commendable. In cases where the draft includes the large audience room, and lecture and Sunday-school room, under the same roof, one may be completed and made to serve the purposes of both, until the necessary money to finish the edifice is fully secured. When the plan calls for a spire, this also may often be left in a rudimentary condition, until the church is paid for, and the means are at hand to complete the plan. This method does not unfurl as many banners, nor set the project before the people with as much tinsel. It will not attract a certain unsettled and unstable class as readily as some other course. But be assured that the better and more serviceable class, who would avoid any church adopting a less prudent course, may, and often are attracted to a new enterprise or growing society by its evident elements of sound financial policy.

The congregations, which, with timid prudence, have involved themselves in greater debt, solely because of their snail-like progress, are so rarely met that they do not form a separate class, and if those who entertain this opinion will take the trouble carefully to investigate, they will find their conclusion in this matter based upon " insufficient reason."

VIII. The indebtedness of some congregations is materially increased because they lack some one to go ahead, who shall feel an abiding personal interest in the prosperity of the church.

Churches, state buildings, railroads, public works and improvements of various kinds are seldom built

as cheaply, as when carried forward as a private enterprise. When exceptions to the rule are found, it is
where some individual has made the interests of the
congregation, state or corporation identical with his
own interests, laboring as faithfully for others as he
would have done for himself. A building committee
may, and frequently does, act so as to secure the best
interests of the congregation, but occasionally they
act as though they were entrusted with the special
duty of creating bills, which the congregation was
entrusted with the special duty of paying.

Some may object to having one act as though building, or financiering for himself, because in numerous
instances this has proven unsatisfactory to the congregation. We reply, that where a committee, or a com-
mittee-man, has grace enough to receive counsel and
good judgment enough to decide which is the better
reason, and religion enough to render his interests
identical with that of the congregation, there is no
reason to question but that it will be by far better to
have one select and purchase, as if for himself, than
to have many, or all, purchase as if for others to pay.

An illustration or two will set forth what we have
sought to say in the two foregoing points. The citizens of a village about five miles from Albany, N. Y.,
determined to build a Methodist church. One of the
prominent citizens, after whom the village is named,

was on the committee appointed to supervise the
entire work. During the winter, when there was little or no demand for building material, and when
dealers were glad to sell at low rates, *for cash*, Mr. S.
went to Albany and purchased the brick required for
the church, purchasing and paying for them as though
he had been purchasing them for himself. The residents of the village and persons living near, having
teams, were notified and requested, when opportunity
permitted, to draw the brick for the new church. In
this way, notwithstanding the railroad conveniences,
the brick were drawn during the winter without a dollar's cost to the congregation. The stones for the
foundation were drawn in the same way, and all the other
needed material being purchased at as reasonable rates
as possible. The work was begun and carried forward in those seasons of the year when the best labor-
ers could be secured at least wages. The church was
some two years in process of erection.

When any one complained because the work was
not hurried forward, it was suggested that money
would do the work, and as fast as it was at hand it
would be applied. All were allowed time to pay their
subscriptions, and many a second subscription. The
result was, that when the church was complete, it was
paid for. It is a fine brick church, having a seating
capacity of about 350, with a Sunday-school room,

class rooms, etc., at the rear, furnished, and all completed at a cost of a fraction less than $10,000, and that at a time when the cost of material and labor was at its height after the war.

A few years later the same congregation built a brick parsonage, with stone trimming, presenting an attractive appearance, being of good size, and having all the conveniences of the most comfortable dwellings in the village. Mr. S. also superintended this building, and completed it at a cost of $1,900.

The Lutheran Church at Shrewsberry, Pa., is a monument of neatness, beauty and cheapness. Built of brick, and having all the improvements and comforts of larger churches, and with a seating capacity of 400, it was completed at a cost of about $12,000, when the cost of material and labor was much higher than at the present time.

The Lutheran Church at Louisville, Ky., is another example, and others might be mentioned, but these suffice to show the result of continual personal supervision.

IX. If one source of church debt is more disheartening than another, it is doubtless that which arises from the disinterestedness of an entire community, or the stinginess of the individual members of a congregation.

Taking the reports of the various denominations of

Christians, noting the amounts contributed for the various benevolences, we discover at once a great diversity existing between different sections of the country. The difference is as marked as the character of the soil, nor are those who inherit the annual laga- cies of the richer soil always the more liberal. This diversity is found not alone in the states, as compared with each other, but in various states there are places where sordid penuriousness and stinginess are provin- cial, affecting all denominations alike. But occa- sionally the ravages of this dreadful distemper are confined to one or more congregations.

It is not necessary, however, to enter into any pro- tracted or minute description of a feature so well known and readily recognized everywhere. We can- not name the difficulty and leave the subject without making a few practical suggestions.

This disease is chronic and obstinate in its charac- ter, and immediate relief can scarce be expected. Sor- did, stingy people will cling to their stinginess as their rarest treasure.

a. The first remedy we would suggest is, to place a church paper in every family, whether members of the church or not. It should be a paper setting forth the interests of the denomination with which the family worships. While a religious paper of some other denomination may be good, it will not render half the service that the organ of one's own church would. Rev. B. B. Collins, missionary of the Lutheran church in India, while collecting funds in this country for missionary purposes, informed us that he found it almost universally true that those families which read the church papers were better informed, and contributed more liberally, while those who did not read the church papers usually gave little or nothing for mission purposes. And every pastor will have observed the same thing in his own congregation.

A church paper will liberalize the minds of its readers in many ways; helping them to know what other congregations are doing, and how they do it; what is expected of church members, and a host of things which the minister could not mention without giving offense.

A good church paper is a great power, and any minister who fails to use it among his people is neglecting one of the great instruments for good. A church paper is the greatest auxiliary and helper which a minister can have in his work.

b. Never preach a " begging sermon." Do not let the people think that God is a beggar, supplicating aid. He is the bountiful giver of all good, and not a beggar. Let giving be set before the people as a means of grace, a Christian duty, a privilege. Rather demand it, than beg for it. But better still, do neither of these. Keep continually before the minds of the people the various wants of the church. Never be scared out of your duty in this, or any other respect. Show the people how God regards the covetous when he classes them with the unrighteous, saying : " Be not deceived ; neither fornicators, nor idolators, nor adulterers, effeminate, nor abusers of themselves with mankind, nor thieves, nor *covetous*, nor drunkards, nor revilers, nor extortioners, shall inherit the kingdom of God." Covetousness is a mean, filthy crime in the sight of God.

c. You cannot hope to accomplish any great results with the generation already having fixed habits. But our source of great power in remedying this whole matter will be found in beginning with the young. Teach them to contribute in the Sunday-school. Not to come with " the niggardly cent," but with dimes, and quarter dollars, and larger amounts. Teach them to contribute regularly, continually, systematically, *religiously.* The parents in their stinginess may find fault, and talk loudly about a free salvation, and all that sort of thing, but never listen to their complaints. Do your duty with the rising generation, building right habits upon right principles, and the result shall abide, whether you shall remain to see it, or another shall come to reap the results of your sowing and toil.

6

X. Some congregations may attribute their growing church debt and diminishing congregations to their own injudicious management, and frequent change of pastors.

What we have to say on this point has already been ably expressed by Mr. Spurgeon, in an address delivered in the Music Hall in Edinburg, in which he gives a very good piece of advice to those who mourn over empty pews and a declining congregation. It is worth trying:

" Sometimes, as the president of a college, I have letters sent to me asking for ministers in something like these terms: ' Dear Sir: Our chapel is very empty ; our last minister was a very excellent man, but an unpopular preacher (I may say, by way of parenthesis, that I suppose he was one of those men that would make good martyrs—so dry that they would burn well), and our congregation is very small. Can you kindly send us a minister who will fill the chapel ?' On one occasion I replied that I had not a minister large enough to fill a chapel. Of course there came an explanation that they did not expect him to corporeally fill it, but to fill it by bringing others to listen to him, and retaining them as seat-holders. Then I wrote, and to gain this opportunity my first joke was perpetrated, reminding the friends that it was quite enough for a pastor to fill the pulpit well, and that the filling of the pews depended upon the zeal, the earnestness, and the diligence of those with whom he commenced his ministry; if they would support him by their earnest co-operation, the meeting-house would soon be full. I remember when I first came to London, preaching to eighty or ninety in a large chapel, but my little congregation thought well of me, and induced others to come and fill the place. I always impute my early success to my warm-hearted people, for they were so earnest and enthusiastic in their loving appreciation of 'the young man from the country' that they were never tired of sounding his praises. If you, any of you, are mourning over empty pews in your place of worship, I would advise you to praise up your minister. There can be no difficulty in discovering some points in which your pastor excels; dwell upon these excellencies, and not upon his failures; talk of the benefit which you derive from his sermons, and thus you will induce the people to come and listen to him, and at the same time you will do him good, for the full house will warm him up and make him a better preacher, and you yourself will enjoy him the more because you have thought and spoken kindly of him. Believe, then, that the filling up of the church is not alone the pastor's work. Remember the word 'universality,' and let no one try to find a loophole to escape his duty. All Christians ought to be doing something for Jesus, and to be always doing something."

XI. Unpaid subscriptions are the cause of some church debts.

Not unfrequently is it the case, that after subscriptions are made, they are forgotten, or the payment neglected. In these cases blame attaches itself, according to circumstances, sometimes to the person subscribing, at other times to the collector, or it may be to the person securing the subscription. Concerning the collections no universal rule can be laid down. Some congregations are composed of men who await the presentation of a bill, while others may be composed of men who so seldom have a bill presented, that when one is presented they will take offense. But in either case, when due public notice has been given, and subscriptions remain unpaid, it is the collector's duty to call upon the parties and request the payment of the same.

But there are cases, also, where congregations become embarrassed because certain subscriptions for large amounts are repudiated. A certain congregation in a large city was induced by a subscription of $5,000, made by the wife of a wealthy merchant in the name of her husband, to incur a large debt. The husband was absent from home at the time, but in consideration of this subscription generous plans were devised and work begun. When the husband returned he refused to pay the subscription. This was the beginning of reverses which almost crushed the congregation with an overpowering debt. There are numerous other cases where subscriptions are made, which, had the parties lived, would have been duly paid. Alienation from the church, loss of property, sickness and death render worthless many subscriptions otherwise good. The safest plan is not to begin the work until a warrantable amount of *money* is already raised.

XII. Some churches become involved in debt by allowing the success of the entire enterprise to rest upon the large liberality of a single individual. Extensive plans and large engagements are entered into, such as the congregation is wholly unable to provide for. Everything may move along prosperously so long as the great supporter of the entire enterprise completes his purpose, but in some evil hour he may meet with financial reverses, and be unable to carry out his cherished plans. "In all such cases the expense should be paid at once, or be provided for in a legal manner, so that if the party or parties concerned should die, change their location, lose their property, or become alienated from the church, the debt may not fall on the masses, who would never have contracted it and are unable to pay or carry it. Our first experience in paying church debts fully justifies this suggestion. The debt was incurred by one good rich man, who controlled in everything and intended to pay it, but was suddenly stricken down by death, leaving no provision, in his will or otherwise, for doing so. His heirs, being opposed to the Methodists, would do nothing. The result was, the debt fell upon a poor society, which struggled under it for many years, expecting to be sold out. Deliverance, however, came at last, but not until several preachers had suffered for want of bread and Methodism had been sadly dishonored.

"This remark is equally applicable to other benevolent enterprises. Gentlemen have liberally proposed to give large sums toward the establishment or endowment of a college or school, and thereby drawn others into the movement; but, failing to pay the amount or give proper security, the whole has been lost, to the damage, if not to the utter defeat of the enterprise. Those who are kind enough to promise such indispensable sums should secure them as fully as they would any just debt for the same amount, otherwise their proposed liberality may prove to be a curse rather than a blessing."*

In fact, large-hearted liberality should be united with great judiciousness, or in many ways it may defeat the worthy motive of its honored projector.

* Rev. James Porter, D. D., in a very excellent book for Methodists, entitled "Helps to Official Members."

The late Gerritt Smith was one of the most generous men in this country. He gave right and left to
almost everyone that came, with little inquiry or dis-
crimination. No doubt his charities relieved a great
deal of suffering and did a great deal of good, but the
good was not unmixed with evil. Perhaps there never
was a more signal illustration of the ill effects of
indiscriminate giving of money. His biographer says
that his prodigal liberality " ruined his beloved Peter-
boro by excessive indulgence, in doing so much for
the villagers, that they became quite incapable of
doing anything for themselves. His generosity dried
up the sources of public spirit and made men posi-
tively sordid. He proposed to build and endow a
library there, and the owners of desirable land-sites
were, all at once, misers, who held the ground at
prices so exorbitant that the scheme was abandoned.
He opened a free reading-room, and the thirst for
information, being anticipated, was discouraged. He
offered to erect a fountain on the common, and the
jealousy of the residents, each of whom wanted it in
front of his own house, caused a bitterness which the
waters of Bethesda could not cure. He presented a
town-clock to the authorities, and they grew at once
so parsimonious that he was requested to provide a
man to wind it up. The common railing was dilapi-
dated, and remained so, because he did not choose to

repair it at his own expense. The brood of parasites increased on this branching oak. Tramps, swindlers and cheats multiplied. Liars sprang up like weeds. Beggars infested the county. His bounty would in many cases, if not in most, have been more wisely bestowed on the devouring sea, which it could not poison, or buried in the ground, where it would lie forever hid."

XIII. Unscriptural motives lead many congregations into situations of great financial embarrassment. Too many churches are built because Mr. Selfwill falls out with the minister, alienates an unstable or impulsive few, and then goes to establish " a church of his own." The question is not, how can the church be made most successful in accomplishing God's great purpose in the redemption of the world, but how can it be made to subserve myself, gratify my selfish ends, and bring honor to my family? Pride, caste, covetousness, self-glory and other unholy motives are allowed too prominent and ruinous a place.

There is also too frequent manifestation of a desire to build a church that will be "an honor to the place," " an ornament to the city," rather than an honor to God. Too many churches are erected to improve the value of adjacent property, for which some have even been stigmatized as the " Church of the Holy Speculation." Too many are built for purely sectarian purposes in localities which could not support the churches already struggling for existence—these, and many other unscriptural ends are too frequently the controlling motives.

CONCLUSION—Other means of getting churches into debt might be named. (*a*) Such as the delusive idea that a church debt is beneficial in binding the congregation together, or giving them something to work for. (*b*.) Contracting with parties who are not responsible, and who may fail in carrying the structure to completion, or loading the edifice with builders' liens, or otherwise embarrass the congregation. (*c*.) Tempting the congregation to build beyond their means by much eloquent talk about getting help from the "Church Extension Society," or "from abroad." This is "like the statesman's promise or the harlot's tears—full of fair seeming, but deception all." (*d*.) By letting "Mr. Highspire, the eminent architect," devise generous plans for spending other people's money, and advertising his own business.

We have sought only to designate the more prevalent sources of this annoying evil. May the church of God be so aroused to realize the enormity of the crime of running in debt, that the free-will offerings of the people shall be as abundant as in the days when the tabernacle was erected in the wilderness, and the

7

workmen came to Moses, saying: " The people being much more than enough for the service of the work which the Lord commanded to make. And Moses gave commandment, and they caused it to be proclaimed throughout the camp, saying, Let neither man nor woman make any more work for the offering of the sanctuary. So the people were restrained from bringing."—(Ex. xxxvi., 5, 6 .

CHAPTER III.

HOW TO PAY CHURCH DEBTS.

DIFFICULTIES IN THE WAY—PREACHING ON THE SUBJECT—
A WRONG POLICY—THE PASTOR'S PART IN PROSECUTING
THE WORK—STOPPING THE EVIL.—CHOICE OF PLAN—
THE SUBSCRIPTION PLAN — DISADVANTAGES — HOW
OVERCOME—FORMS OF—SELECTING A COMMITTEE—SUG-
GESTIONS TO COMMITTEES—MAKING COLLECTIONS—
NOTE SUBSCRIPTION — ADVANTAGES — DIFFICULTIES—
LAW CONCERNING—SUGGESTIONS—FORMS, &c.—TAX-
LIST PLAN—ADVANTAGES—OBJECTIONS—APPORTIONING
PLAN—SHARE PLAN—ENVELOPE SUBSCRIPTION PLAN—
SINKING-FUND PLAN—HELPING PLAN—PASTORAL LET-
TER PLAN—SAMPLES OF—MONTHLY COLLECTION PLAN
— MORTGAGE DONATION PLAN — APPEALS THROUGH
CHURCH PAPERS—CANVASSING OTHER CONGREGATIONS
—THE DEFRAUDING PLAN—FAIRS, CONCERTS, &c.—GOD'S
PLAN—ARE THE CHURCHES ABLE TO PAY THE DEBTS?

There are plenty of people, members of the Christian Church, who could any day pay off the debts
which curse the Church and impede its progress, and
not lose a single meal, or deprive themselves of a
single comfort. There is no lack of ability, but a lack
of desire and even of willingness to perform a clear
and unmistakable duty. How shall this difficulty be
overcome?

PREACHING ON THE SUBJECT.

Let the scriptural duty of making ample provision for God's house be fully set forth from the pulpit. Don't beg, don't scold. Preach the whole counsel of God, not evading the ordained law of the giving of the tithe, a law which was not made for the Jew, but was enjoined about two thousand years before Abraham was born—a law that is as old as the institution of sacrifice, as old as the institution of the Sabbath, and as universal as the human race—a law which could as justly be called *heathen*, as *Jewish*, for its binding force is recognized to-day in every heathen country, and it stands out unmistakably as one of the landmarks which leads the nations back to a common origin and a divine revelation—a law which, be it said to our shame, is observed in every heathen nation, and is violated only by those who call themselves Christians.

We say, then, preach upon this subject. Let the scriptural view of God as the great proprietor, and man as the steward, be faithfully set forth. Let human responsibility and accountability be faithfully enjoined, not simply in the use of intellectual culture and power, but in the use of material wealth. In the parable of the talents it was property, MONEY, which was intrusted, and for which each had to give an account. There is no escaping from the truth presented in this scripture.

Men are enjoined to give at *least* a tenth for the support and spread of the gospel. One-tenth is the Lord's and the remaining nine-tenths is his also, and we are simply to *use* it as his stewards. As we may not withhold the one-tenth, neither may we squander the remainder in undue luxury and pride. Our wealth is to be sanctified wealth.

Let pastors entrusted with congregations burdened with church debts present these truths, not only in an occasional discourse, but frequently. Let them familiarize themselves with this neglected doctrine until it shall form as much a part of all their teachings, as it forms a part of each book, and runs through every chapter of the Bible. Let pastor and people together confess their sin in this matter, and prove their sincerity by bringing their free-will offerings and paying their debt. Remember! the tithe is God's money, sacredly set apart for the support and spread of the gospel, so do not let the people take God's money to pay *their* debt. Let the *people's* money pay the *people's* debt. Free-will offerings are what God requires for this purpose; so let the rich give liberally from their abundance, and let the poor from the depths of their poverty enjoy the same blessed privilege. Let there be an enlightened and quickened conscience, and we know that the Christian men and women of this land will arise and cast off the burdens with which the church is now struggling to go forward.

A WRONG POLICY.

Many pastors pursue a ruinous policy. They think that all contributions for benevolent work at home, or the spread of the gospel abroad, should be merged into the fund for local support. The heathen must care for themselves, and every noble charity must be forsaken to make provision for current expenses, and to " get ready to pay the debt." It is a great mistake ! You might as well stop the throbbing of the heart in order to increase the strength of the physical man. In stopping the benevolent contributions and work of the church, you will be killing every generous impulse, and destroying the very motives which should only be quickened and strengthened if the debt is ever to be paid at all.

A certain congregation in a small village had a debt of nearly $25,000. The pastor advocated giving to every worthy object which appealed for aid. In three years $19,000 of the great debt was cancelled, no worthy suppliant was turned away empty, the church had risen in the amount of its contributions for missions, and the various agencies of the church, until it occupied the second place in the Synod with which it stood connected. The succeeding pastor, with a debt of $7,000, pursued a policy directly the reverse, and at the end of his second year had the effrontery to stand upon the floors of Synod, and offer as an excuse for not having raised a single dollar for missions, nor any of the agencies of the church, " that he had told his people from the pulpit that they should contribute nothing for these objects, as they needed all their money at home to pay the debt." What was the result of such a policy? As might naturally be expected, the congregation had not paid current expenses, they had not paid a single dollar on the debt, nor had they even paid the interest of the debt.

" We may learn a better wisdom from the example of one of the wisest pastors in New York City. When his church was being built, the question of establishing a mission school came before his people. After much debate, the pastor rose to speak on the subject. He detailed the account of their circumstances, showed that they were building a costly church, that they had a heavy burden of debt coming upon them, and, in short, as much as they could bear. ' Therefore,' said he—and every person thought his conclusion was easy to see, supposing he would add at once—' therefore we cannot afford a mission school ;' but his wisdom rose an octave above that commonplace reasoning of men, and with an inspiration of the truth as to God's laws in the church, he added : ' Therefore we cannot afford to be without a mission school.' The great church built to-day, the mission school established, and both prosperous, show the blessing on that deep insight into the facts of God's government in the world."*

PASTOR'S PART IN THE WORK.

Every pastor of a debt-burdened people has often asked himself the question, What part shall I take in this work ? Shall I carry the subscription, or shall I intrust it to a committee ? Is the minister to be like the general who in the day of battle neglects the more responsible duties of commander for the sake of rendering service as a private? Will not the pastor render more valuable service in the capacity of a supervisor, or director, making efficient the labors of many, rather than by entering the field as an individual laborer? Is it not a wicked perversion of the ordinance of God to take ministers from the sacred work of their pulpits and pastorates to do the work of gathering, and ofttimes of *begging* funds from the very ones who should come of themselves and pay the debt which they have contracted and promised to pay ? Are they not Christ's embassadors rather than the people's beggars ? Are they not sent to preach the everlasting gospel, to reclaim the lost, to perfect the saints, to edify the body of Christ? And is it right that they should be turned from this high and holy work to that of circulating a subscription, or soliciting funds ?

*Rev. John Abbott French, in "Giving in Hard Times."

But there are other questions also which enter into the consideration. If there is no one else to carry the subscription and act the part of solicitor, shall the pastor refuse to perform the duty and allow the cause to fail? Is not the minister as much responsible for the success of the financial as the spiritual interests of the church? If the ranks are breaking, and men are scattering, may not the situation require the commander to ride to the very front, and assuming the duties of the rank and file, become an inspiration to his host? If the people have failed to discharge their duty to God, may it not be because their duty has not been fully and forcibly presented? If the church has fallen into the pit, who could more appropriately help it out, than the minister? Was not Peter, when he went fishing to secure money to pay taxes, as truly and fully in Christ's service, as when he "lifted up his voice" on the day of Pentecost?

These and many other questions present themselves upon either side. Our own course has been, never to allow the cause to fail for want of some one to go ahead and do this arduous and unpleasant work. The question is a difficult one, and no definite rule can be prescribed. In earnest prayer, relying upon God to determine the question of duty, each one must seek divine direction.

8

STOPPING THE EVIL.

After the debt has been paid, "the first thing to be done," says Rev. William Ramsey, "is to prevent any further increase of the evil. If the churches which are now involved in debt should be relieved, and if nothing be done to stop this iniquitous system of building churches without paying for them, we shall make but slow progress in this work of reform. It certainly would not show much. wisdom in the friends of temperance if they should spend all their energies in trying to reform drunkards, without aiming to prevent another generation of them from rising up to be a scourge and a curse to society. The young must be kept sober, or they will become drunkards. So it is with church debts. If we pay off the existing debts of the churches, and still countenance the sin of building new churches without paying for them, we shall soon have the same evil to mourn over that we now have. The practice must be resolutely frowned upon by every lover of the church of Christ. Let no church be erected through vain glory or party spirit, or to gratify the pride or feelings of a few. But let them be erected only when and where they are needed. And let them be paid for before ever a Christian minister shall, in the name of the people, stand up in their presence and dedicate to God that which they know does not belong to them. This evil may easily be prevented. It is in the power of the ministers to do it at once. Let them resolve that they will not dedicate a church to God that is in debt, and that they will not destroy the comfort and peace of a brother, and hinder his usefulness, by placing him over a church that is in debt, and soon the evil complained of will be cured. If this were done, we should seldom hear of ministers leaving their people for want of a support. The members of the churches would then understand what they must do to have a minister of Christ placed over them; and when they had him, they would be free to labor for the salvation of souls, without the continued annoyance of a debt. I might ask you now to look at the churches in this city (Philadelphia , and to tell me what it is which perplexes the minds of the officers of the churches. It is their debt. What breaks in upon the studies and pastoral duties of the settled pastors? The church debt. What turns off the minds of the elders and leading men of the church from the great work of saving souls? It is their church debt. What is it that leads the people to lessen the salary of their ministers, or to fix it at the lowest possible rate, or to be always dilatory in paying their ministers, so that he is often pressed beyond measure for the mere necessities of life? It is the church debt. What is it that brings down the curse of God upon

the churches throughout our land? It is the awful
fact that they are robbing God of his due. Do you
ask, wherein do they rob him? I answer 'In tithes
and offerings.' It surely is not the time for those
who call themselves the stewards of God to be dwell-
ing in their ceiled houses, while the house of God
remains unfinished or in debt. May the churches
have grace to 'consider their ways,' and repent of the
great evil, that the blessing of God may rest upon
them!"

CHOICE OF PLAN.

No one plan is equally well suited to meet the requirements of all parishes. Each pastor, or committee, must select such a one as comes nearest to meeting their wants, and then modify until all difficulties
are overcome. In raising a *debt*, more will depend
upon the plan used, and the prudence of the committee, than in securing money for a new enterprise.
Yet it is well to add, that too much importance is not
to be attached to the plan. A fixed method is necessary, and a good plan is much to be preferred to a
poor one, yet no plan will of itself do the work, or pay
the debt. A plan may be like a mechanical contri-
vance for applying power for the accomplishment of
a desired result. It may be so rudely constructed, or
be so deficient in many of its parts that there will be
great loss of motive power; or, it may be constructed

with the greatest nicety of adjustment, and be deficient only in wanting the *power* necessary to accomplish the desired result. A poorly chosen plan may greatly hinder, or even defeat the efforts of the most judicious committee, and upon the other hand, a plan may be faultless, but be so poorly worked, that it would be impossible for it to produce anything but failure.

"The best mode of securing contributions is not necessarily that which secures, in every instance, the largest contributions, but that which gives play to the grace of beneficence in the greatest number, and which secures cheerfulness and intelligent satisfaction in the act of the donors. In the long run, this method will also be found to secure the largest contributions."

One very desirable feature in any plan is, that it should render it easy for the people to see how the amount needed may easily be raised by united effort. The plan should not only itself be simple, but should also simplify the payment of the debt. To its simplicity it should add efficiency.

SUBSCRIPTION PLAN.

Perhaps no plan has been more generally used in this century than the well-known form of subscription. It has some advantages and some disadvantages. The principal trouble with the subscription plan is that it affords no reliable guarantee that the amounts

subscribed will ever be paid. In the minds of many
people it is too lightly regarded. While the subscriptions can be collected by law, yet we have never known
one to be thus collected. Dr. Porter mentions a case
in which $27,000 was subscribed, and less than $6,000
was ever paid. There are always too many conditions
suffered to enter into the subscription plan. Too long
a time is allowed to elapse between the date of the
subscription and the date of payment. Persons may
lose their zeal, or become offended, or estranged, and
seek occasion for finding fault, or excuse for not paying. In these and various other ways the losses on
subscriptions often lead to serious embarrassment.

In order to overcome these difficulties it would be
well to make the subscription more explicit than is
usually done. It should always specify when the
various amounts pledged shall be payable, and to
whom they shall be paid. The object for which the
money is to be raised should be clearly stated, and all
the conditions should be incorporated in full. "If
any subscription is to be paid otherwise than in cash,
this should be stated. All fictitious subscriptions
obtained for the purpose of inducing others to subscribe, or to subscribe more largely, invalidate all
that follow them. If the object proposed shall not be
undertaken, the subscription is not binding."*

*Rev. James Porter, D. D.

FORMS OF SUBSCRIPTION.

No specified form is necessary to render a subscription legal. They may be variously constructed to suit the requirements of the case. We give a couple of forms :

—————, N. Y., Oct. 1st, 1880.

We, the undersigned, members and friends of Trinity Lutheran Church, do hereby subscribe and agree to pay the amounts set opposite our respective names, for the purpose of erecting a new church edifice, the same to be constructed of brick, the cost, when completed, not to exceed $35,000, the same to be all subscribed and one-half paid into the hands of the trustees before ever the contracts shall be awarded or the work begun. The amounts of the various subscriptions are to be paid to the trustees in two equal installments ; the first installment shall be payable as soon as the entire amount necessary shall have been subscribed, and the second installment six months thereafter. Should the conditions stated above not be complied with, the various subscriptions shall be null and void.

Another Form.

We, the undersigned, severally agree to pay to the Treasurer of the First Presbyterian Church the sum set opposite our respective names for the purpose of liquidating the debt and paying the mortgage upon the parsonage of said church, one-half on demand, and the balance three months after the demand for the first payment.

————————Pa., September 12, 1880.

SELECTING A COMMITTEE.

Where the method to be used is such as to require a soliciting or canvassing committee, the greatest care is to be exercised in the selection. They should be of such (*a.*) as are willing to inconvenience themselves, forego pleasure, lay aside their own business, and give the necessary amount of time to this important work. (*b.*) They should be such as have the success of the undertaking at heart. (*c.*) They should be only of such as contribute (whether the amount be much or little) to the *full extent* of their ability. Then their influence will be salutary, and their words have weight with others. (*d.*) They must be persons of influence because of their consistent Christian lives. (*e.*) They should be persons not easily disheartened, or soon discouraged. (*f.*) Should be such as are not of hasty temper, easily provoked to anger, or given to injudicious speech. (*g.*) If possible, avoid the selection of all such as are odd, eccentric, morose, long-faced, fault-finding, repulsive, overbearing, dictatorial.

SUGGESTIONS TO COMMITTEES.

You will see by the foregoing something of what you should at least seek to be, if you would be fitted for the important work for which you have been chosen. A few additional suggestions may be of service.

1. The first thing necessary is to secure a complete list of all persons who should subscribe something. Do not slight the poor, nor forget the women, nor such young persons as are earning money. No members of the family should be slighted, not even the children.

2. As nearly as possible, learn what amount each person on the list would be able to contribute, and apportion the entire amount to be raised among the various individuals. If the committee cannot apportion it, they will not be likely to raise it. In going to the various parties it will be found necessary occasionally to increase or diminish the amount, but it will serve a very excellent guage.

3. Much caution must be exercised to prevent penurious persons from escaping by subscribing some trifling and insufficient amount. It might be better to leave such persons until the last, rather than have the subscriptions of others decreased because of the niggardliness of such individuals. The cause would really succeed better without them, than with them, if the rest of the congregation could only see it in that light.

4. Always regard with suspicion all hints, insinua-

9

tions, and offers of liberal help upon uncertain conditions, but which cannot be reduced to a *bona-fide* subscription.

5. If the subscription is started with the understanding that a certain amount is to be raised, or the subscribtion is to become null and void, there may be some, as has elsewhere been the case, who, in a moment of zeal or personal pride, will pledge more than they subsequently think best, and then openly, or secretly, exert themselves to defeat the success of the effort. Much patience and prudence are needed in dealing with such individuals.

6. " The subscription book should specify when the several sums pledged shall be due and payable, and it is generally wise to have them divided into installments to accommodate the maturing liabilities of the trustees or building committee growing out of the contract. People in ordinary circumstances can pay a subscription in three or four installments, several weeks or months apart, easier than they can pay the whole at once. And, if the subscribers understand that these payments are arranged to accommodate the obligations of the trustees to the builder, they will be much more likely to pay promptly."

7. As the securing of funds for liquidating a debt, or carrying forward a new enterprise, is only a means to an end, viz: that the church may become more effi-

cient in saving souls and rendering men better, be very careful what means you use to secure the subscriptions. Do not quicken such passions as the gospel of Christ is designed to allay. Do not appeal to pride, vain glory, selfishness, or a spirit of emulation, and leave the religious affections unawakened, or but partially enlisted in this great work. Touch the main-spring appointed of God to move the soul in the performance of duty in this matter. Place the main reliance on the main motive—the heart. Let your appeals be such that each subscriber shall be rendered better in proportion as you enable him to see his duty, and induce him to contribute from scriptural motives and religious principles.

8. Frequent reports should be publicly made to the congregation. As all who contribute are sure to become more interested in the success of the undertaking, they will always be anxious to learn what progress the committee is making. The report of the committee, with the names of subscribers and amounts pledged, may be read each Sabbath by the pastor, when making the various announcements for the week, or printed reports may be distributed through the congregation gratuitously. Every member of the congregation is a partner in the business, and should be kept informed in regard to all that is being done by the committee. It is a great mistake to keep the

subscriptions secret, or fail to report how the money is disbursed. Fair, open-handed dealing is by far the best, both for the success of the undertaking and the protection of the committee.

MAKING COLLECTIONS.

On the subject of collecting the subscriptions, Rev. James Porter, D. D., very aptly remarks :

"We advise, also, that payment be kindly and promptly demanded as in every other business, and of each and every subscriber. Trustees who can readily command funds on their own personal credit are apt to neglect this. They often collect the larger sub-scriptions in full, and leave the smaller ones to the last, which gives the impression to the young and poor that they are not considered of much account. This is a double mistake, *first*, in that it increases the lia-bility of losing the small subscriptions altogether : and, *secondly*, in that it lets an opportunity slip of impressing the poor that their subscriptions, however small, are appreciated, and that they are partners in the noble enterprise. This large class of our members and friends have enough, at the least, to discourage them, and should have the benefit of all such atten-tions, for their own good, and that of the cause when they shall become more able. Few fully appreciate the importance of keeping such people in good spirits. Young ——— subscribed five dollars toward erecting the first little church in his native town, and raised the money by trapping musk-rats, and felt the better for it, and for the manner in which it was received. When that church was superseded by a better one, a splendid edifice, he gave many thousands. Had his first noble liberality been despised, the result might have been less gratifying.

" We say, then, collect the small subscriptions promptly and kindly. Let little Tommy pay his, and Mary hers, and the old folks theirs, and make them feel they are important spokes in the wheel of progress. This will justify you in pressing your claims upon another class everywhere found, who have more means, but are constitutionally tardy, especially in paying church subscriptions."

NOTE SUBSCRIPTION PLAN.

For some years past the note subscription plan has largely superseded the old form of general subscription. In some respects it is much to be preferred.

1. It suffers but a very small percentage of loss, resulting from unpaid pledges. While in the eyes of the law it is no more binding than a subscription, yet in the minds of the people it has greater weight.

2. The note system easily provides for the interest, and when the amounts equivalent to the entire debt are once pledged, the debt becomes virtually removed from the church, and is distributed among the various

subscribers, for if they are not able to pay at once, the interest of the one will meet the interest of the other. This feature is a very excellent one, for the providing for the interest of a debt is a very trouble-some matter.

3. It more readily allows of payments in regular installments. The whole amount of the donation may be divided equally, or unequally, into *separate* notes, all drawn at the same time, and then, as each is paid, it is torn off, and returned to the drawer, in place of a receipt. Or, the various installments may be endorsed on the back of the note until the last payment is made, when it is returned to the drawer.

4. The "stub," which remains after the note is torn off, serves an excellent purpose in preserving a com-plete and convinient record of the entire subscription, giving the date of the note, face of note, interest, total amount, drawer of the note, to whom it was paid, and when paid.

5. The notes may be drawn up in regular bank form, and be discounted in event of needing money to meet accruing obligations, or they may simply be left at the bank for payment or collection.

They may also have, in some instances, a couple of difficulties, or objections.

1. The note subscription allows of no conditions. If the payments are to be made upon certain condi-

tions, these conditions may be in verbal or written contract (not under seal), but must not be expressed either in the body of the note, or upon the back. A promissory note must be clogged by no conditions or contingencies. To be a legal note " It must be for the payment of money *at all events,* and hence if there be any contingency as to its payment, it is no bill or note. But if made payable on the happening of an event, however remote, yet if it be of *certain occurrence,* the bill or note is good, as if made payable two months after the death of the maker's father.

"Conditions to destroy the character of a bill or note need not be on its face. An endorsement on the back of it, rendering it payable upon certain conditions, and *done at the time of the making of it,* will have the same effect. But a contemporaneous *parol** agreement can have no such effect, because, resting in parol, it is not admissible in evidence, nor would an endorsement which simply referred to an agreement by way of identification."†

2. Some persons will object to placing their names to a note. These may usually be met by showing them that the nature of the regular subscription is such as to render it equally as binding as a note; or that it is the form upon which the congregation have

---

*Parol contract —"Any contract not of record or under seal, whether oral or written ; a simple contract."—*Story.*

†Bryant & Stratton's "Commercial Law," § 285 and § 286.

agreed for the mere sake of uniformity ; or, if no other alternative presents itself, such persons may be allowed to pledge their amounts upon a regular subscription, in which it is also agreed to pay the interest upon the amount subscribed. Generally, though not always, this excuse is a mere *pretext*, to escape the payment of any subscription at all.

SUGGESTIONS.

All subscribers should have a clear understanding of what disposition is to be made of their notes. If the trustees, or the parties to whom they are made payable, propose to sell the notes, or use them in paying bills, this should be clearly understood by each person before signing the note. They should know where they may find their note, and to whom the money is to be paid. If they are to be discounted, or left at the bank for collection, this should be distinctly understood, or unpleasant results may come of such a course ; but where this is agreed upon, and named in the note, it may, at least among business men, be the more pleasant method of disposing of the matter.

The notes and stubs may be easily and cheaply bound in flexible covers, about a hundred in a book. This will be a neat and convenient form, and then when the notes are all paid and torn off, the cover may be reduced to the size of the stubs, and this will preserve them in permanent form for future reference.

Date of Note   188
Face of Note $
Interest $
Total $
Drawer
Paid to
When Paid

Date of Note   188
When Due   188
Face of Note $
Interest $
Total amount $
Drawer
When Paid

$ Cobleskill, N. Y.,   188

after date I promise to pay to the Trustees of ZION'S EVANGELICAL LUTHERAN CHURCH, of Cobleskill, N. Y., or order,

Dollars,

with interest, value received.

$ Easton, Pa.,   188

after date promise to pay to the order of the Trustees of St. Paul's Lutheran Church at the FIRST NATIONAL BANK OF EASTON,

Dollars,

with interest, without defalcation. Value received.

It may not be out of place for us to say, just here, that it pays many fold to have all the envelopes, notes and various papers needed in church work, neatly printed. Printers' ink, judiciously used, pays well in every business enterprise, and it has proven equally valuable in the successful management of churches. Notes can be printed and bound for about seventy-five cents or a dollar a hundred, and to undertake to use this system without printed notes would end in confusion, and perhaps disgust.

TAX-LIST PLAN.

In paying a debt, some congregations have resorted to the assessor's book, or the amounts fixed in the tax list in order to secure an equitable division of the entire amount among the various parties who should contribute. At first thought this plan is likely to be regarded with favor, and we have known an instance or two in which it has really been used with success, but the difficulties which encompass it are so numerous, that it more generally gives place to some other system. If the town or city taxes are regarded as equitable and justly apportioned among the various residents, then it may not be difficult to secure the assent of the congregation, for the introduction of the plan, but if this is not felt to be the case, such assent will not readily be obtained. It will not do to adopt it unless it is received with unanimous favor.

The majority may not inflict this upon the minority without invading their rights. They may urge it as a standard of duty, but they have no right to enforce it as an inflexible law. God has made us free moral agents, and no body of men, either in church or state, have delegated to them the right to deprive us of that freedom. To this, however, there is a limit. In the sight of God covetousness is as great a crime as lying or theft, and when the church shall have washed her hands clean from this great sin of "*covetousness which is idolatry*," then it may eject its members for this as well as for any other heresy.

Dr. Lansing, a missionary in Egypt, tells us that a native deacon at Stuft, sixty miles south of Cairo, suspended ten of his members for such things as bad dispositions, vanity, stinginess and not allowing their wives to go to weekly prayer meetings. What a thinning out there would be if such things were permitted to have weight here. And yet, why should not the church in some way take notice of bad tempers, biting tongues, stinginess and all the impish brood of vices and habits that are practically not considered incompatible with "professed" religion?

We have, however, known an instance in which this plan was adopted by an almost unanimous vote, but there were two members who dissented, and subsequently refused to pay the amounts apportioned to them. They were arraigned before the Church Council, tried, and their names stricken from the roll of membership. The case was appealed, carried up to the Synod, and the action reversed.

ADVANTAGES.—The tax-list plan is simple, easily comprehended, and if it can be adopted with unanimous consent, the labor of securing the amount necessary may be greatly reduced. But it is apt meet with various

OBJECTIONS.—1. That the tax-list itself is not equitable, and does not justly indicate the financial strength of the various persons enrolled.

2. There are many nominally poor people, who would give liberally, whose names do not appear at all upon the tax-list.

3. Many persons who are nominally rich, and are large tax-payers, are "property poor," and have little or no ready money.

4. It has the appearance of being, although it need not really be, less scriptural than various other plans. The contributions seem to have too little of the liberal, "willing mind" spirit which the Bible everywhere inculcates. The various contributors are apt to appear as though they were fearful lest they should, by any accident, contribute a single dollar more than equity, or absolute necessity demanded, and it is at least questionable whether the tendencies are not

toward such a result. "The Lord loveth a *cheerful* giver."

APPORTIONING PLAN.

A plan, kindred to the tax-list plan, and a modification of it, might be called the apportioning plan. It consists in selecting a judicious committee, whose duty it shall be to acquaint themselves, by any reasonable means, with the pecuniary ability of all who may be expected to contribute, and then to apportion the debt in an equitable and just manner among them. The results of the committee's work, if the whole debt be very large, may be reported in full to the congregation, for their sanction, or, if the entire amount be less imposing, the congregation may decide at the time of appointment, that they will abide by the judgment of the committee.

In many congregations this plan has worked very satisfactory results. It is devoid of most of the difficulties and objections which are inherent in the tax-list plan.

After the committee have completed the apportionment, each of the members and friends of the congregation may be informed of the amount they are expected to pay by a circular letter. A suggestive form will be found under the head of "The Envelope System " in Chapter IV.

SHARE PLAN.

The plan of dividing the entire amount of the debt into equal portions, and calling them shares, has worked well in many parishes. This may be illustrated by an example or two. A Presbyterian church in the state of Wisconsin had a debt of $1,000. This amount was divided into 274 shares, of $3.65 each, and was taken by 130 persons. Thirty shares, amounting to $109.50, was the largest number taken by any one individual. The others ranged from that number down to a single share.

In some instances it may be a good idea to arrange the supporters of the church, according to wealth and modifying circumstances, into four, five, or more classes, and then apportion a uniform number of shares to each individual of the same class. This may aid in making the final amount adequate to pay the entire debt, for one of the disheartening results of raising a debt is to canvass the entire field, and then, at the last, to find that there still remains a balance unprovided for.

Where the amount to be raised is larger, the shares may be divided into sums of $12, or $24, or $50, or more, and then be paid in regular installments of $1, $2, or $5, weekly, semi-monthly or monthly, as the committee may see fit. The amounts may be paid to the treasurer direct, or placed in a sealed envelope and deposited in the collection basket each Sabbath as a free-will offering.

Where the execution of this plan is entrusted into the hands of a judicious and persevering committee, there is little or no reason why it should not be rendered a success. In well-to-do congregations, it is best suited to the liquidation of the smaller indebtednesses; but where the entire membership is composed of persons of but limited means, it will be found very serviceable in enab ing them to provide for a large amount, by extending the payments over a greater period of time.

ENVELOPE SUBSCRIPTION PLAN.

This plan differs from the regular subscription, in that the payments are made weekly, or monthly, in envelopes, instead of the entire amount being paid in one or two installments at greater intervals. It differs also from the share plan in that the amounts are unprescribed.

After the amounts have been subscribed, each contributor is supplied with the necessary number of envelopes, the form of which may be suggested by the following:

Remember the Lord thy God, for it is He that giveth thee power to get wealth.--*Deut. viii.*, 18.

Register No.   *Am't Enclosed* $

FREE-WILL OFFERING.

From

Contributed toward the liquidation of the church debt.

☞ *Enclose the amount* REGULARLY, *seal, and place in the collection basket.*

This plan may be combined with the regular envelope system used to provide for current expenses. In making the annual assessment for current expenses, the interest and a portion of the principal may be added, and the entire amount apportioned among the members and supporters of the church. The amounts are placed together in the same envelope, and deposited in the basket, to be credited by the treasurer to the specified objects, or, the contents may be credited in one amount, out of which fund current expenses may be paid, and the balance remaining at the end of the year, appropriated to pay interest and reduce the debt. This latter, however, is not as business-like as the former, and is apt to be attended with more loss on account of unpaid subscriptions, or using all the funds to meet current expenses, investments and losses.

SINKING-FUND PLAN.

Where a congregation is composed of such as have no accumulated property, but are dependent upon their daily labor, it is well to use a sinking-fund plan. This consists in the appropriation of an annual surplus to the reduction of the debt. It may be a plan like the preceding envelope subscription, or it may be an annual surplus from pew rentals, or any other revenue the church may have.

A very good plan was tried by Rev. G. W. Enders, and by request of the editor of the *Lutheran Evan-*

gelist, was written up for publication in that paper. As it is full of energy and suggestion, we insert it here in full :

" Mr. Editor :

" I propose to fulfill my promise by writing, at your request, an article of our method of paying our church debt. It is one of the good signs of the times that churches are bestirring themselves to be up with the apostolic injunction, 'owe no man anything.'

" I found every church, of which I have been pastor, in debt My experience bears me out in saying that a debt is one of the most serious hindrances to the prosperity of the church. Does the pastor want to make any local improvement, or take up a collection for missions or any other benevolent cause, he is met with, ' But we must pay off the debt first, charity begins at home,' &c. But that debt is carefully preserved to furnish excuse against charity anywhere.

" Well, I found my present church in debt about $4,000. My first endeavor after settlement here was to pay the debt. But various " I pray thee have me excused,' met me at every turn. Some said, ' Can't be done these hard times,' others, ' We've paid our share already, let others pay up;' others, ' We've paid to the church for years, now let this debt alone and our children will pay it when they grow up,' and others still pleaded, ' It 's not good for a church to be out of

11

debt, because so long as a church has debt it won't go into new undertakings and expense-, and so money is saved by having a debt,' etc.

"I found it, therefore, impractible to pay off our church debt in the usual way. I cast about, resolved upon and carried out, and 'propose to continue the following plan, viz:

"I districted my congregation by streets and squares in the city, and those in the county by neighborhoods. All this I put on paper.

"Then I called a meeting of all my young people and all *unmarried* communicants, excluding everybody else. To this assembly my plan was submitted, with suitable instructions and explanations. A young people's society was immediately organized, the young ladies electing one of their number as treasurer for their portion of the lot. Similarly a young man was elected treasurer for the young men. Collectors were appointed in every district according to my written programme, and it was agreed that each one ought to give at least one cent a day towards the payment of the debt, and the collectors were instructed to make a list of all church members within their respective districts, and to call regularly *once* every week for contributions. My young people took hold of this work with enthusiasm, and with what result the conclusion will show.

"Next I called a meeting of all the married ladies of the congregation and proposed my plan. They adopted it and at once proceeded to appoint collectors to make the weekly collection.

"Then I organized my Catechetical class, in like manner electing a girl and boy respectively, treasurer for their sides, and one exercise of the meeting of the class was to *take up the collection wherever the class met.* Next, younger children were appointed in various parts of the congregation to gather the children's offerings. (But to date I have been unable to see my way clear to organize the *fathers* into active companies.)

"During the last week of each month the collectors report to their respective treasurers and pay over the money. Then on the first Sunday in the month a service appropriate is held in the church, and each treasurer and all persons wishing to make gifts are invited to arise and bring their offering to the altar and lay it thereon, after which a general collection is held for this same object.

"We began this work last January, and have not omitted a single week or month. Of course, it requires tact, care and labor to keep so extensive a machinery in running order. Feeble objections, and sometimes obstructions arise, but a little oil prevents much friction. But some will say, ' What, a penny a day, and

every day, week and month ?   It's too silly, and won't
work or it won't pay.'   Well, to satisfy all such, let
me say that I esteem it to be God's plan, ' here a little and there a little.'

"And I give you here the monthly results.   We
began about the middle of January, and the first Sunday in

Febraary was our first collection..........$ 80 27
March............................... 231 02
April................................ 136 80
May................................. 124 13
June (including $100 given by one member). 208 34
July.................................   64 65
August............................... 112 16
September (including $207 15 from railroad
    excursion)........................ . 291 37

"Moreover, several hundred dollars of old sub
scriptions have during this time been paid which were
considered void, but these regular collections stirred
and quickened several consciences into financial recti-
tude.

" The result among my people is universal satisfaction with this method.   All give regularly, and no
one feels as if he had been injured by giving too
much.   All is voluntary.   Our collections for other
general benevolence have increased in spite of hard
times.   And in July my people felt that this plan was
working such admirable results that they took cour-

age to build a parsonage, which is now under roof; we like our plan so well that we shall keep on till the old debt and parsonage are paid for.

"And now, my dear brother pastor, is your church in debt? Then try faithfully our plan, and ' despise not the day of small things,' and you will be more than gratified with results.

"———— Ind.   GEO. W. ENDERS."

As these plans are likely to extend through a series of years, they are apt to weary both those who contribute and those who have the matter in charge. The result, however, is good, in that it enables a congregation to cancel its indebtedness, and tends to discipline a congregation in constant giving, and then, when the debt is paid, they will more naturally contribute toward other objects worthy of aid.

HELPING PLAN.

Rev. William Ramsey, in considering how weak, struggling congregations may be enabled to pay their disheartening debts, suggests the following:

"It can be done in a short time, by a number of Christians, who are not needed in the larger and wealthier churches, uniting their contributions, efforts and prayers with those who are laboring in the feebler churches. In this manner they will obey the injunction of the apostle, who said, 'I have showed you all things, how that so laboring ye ought to support the weak ;' and to remember the words of the Lord Jesus, when he said, 'It is more blessed to give than to receive.'

"I will illustrate my meaning by a case which is worthy of being recorded. There are, I trust, many like it. May there be many more. It is this: In conversing with Mr. K., a worthy member of the Methodist church, the following dialogue took place:

"I—'Where now do you attend church?'

"K.—'I attend the Wharton-street Church.'

"I—'When did you go there?'

"K.—'I will tell you. You know we built a church there some time ago. We had a very good minister, but, as the population was very much scattered, and there were but few members, the church did not prosper. It was then proposed that a number of members from the city churches should go and aid them. About two hundred of us volunteered to go. Some go as far as two miles or more, every Sabbath and through the week. I have been there about two years. Our coming inspired the minister and the people with new zeal. We went to work, and we have now a membership of about six hundred.'

"I—'Well, my friend, you adopted the right plan, and if other weak churches could be aided in the same way, they might prosper, too.'

"K.—'No doubt of it. Feeble churches need something else besides money.'

"I—'I suppose that you are not sorry that you have left your old church, to labor there?'

"K.—'No, sir. We have seen some precious times there. But, as they are pretty strong now, some of us are drawing off, with the intention of aiding some other feeble church.'

"I—'Go on in your good work, my brother, and may the Lord prosper you!'

"We shook hands and parted.

"Now, something like this might be done with the greatest ease imaginable, for every feeble church. Yea, more, it ought to be done; and the word of the Lord would have free course and be glorified. But will Christians do so? Probably not. But the time will come, when God shall raise up another generation of Christians, who will possess a different spirit."

PASTORAL LETTER PLAN.

Where the people are fully awake to the duty of giving, no easier, more convenient, or efficient plan can be used than the printed circular, or pastoral letter plan. It does away with all undue pressure, unscriptural arguments, personal appeal, and personal influence. The success of the plan is made to rest, not upon impulse, but upon conscience and principle. This was the method used by St. Paul in collecting the *alms* of the Christians at Corinth to aid the poor and persecuted Christians of Judea. They were not to wait until the apostle stood before them in person, and with an appeal of moving oratory or tender pathos, played upon their emotions and secured their contributions, but they were to give from principle—from a sense of Christian duty—laying by in store as God had prospered them, that there be no solicitation and no personal appeals when the apostle should come.

Much might be said in favor of this method. It must, however, be distinctly understood that its success is dependent upon *an enlightened sense of Christian duty.* If this is wanting, but little can be expected to result from the use of the pastoral letter plan.

We have known this method to be used with great success, and in an enlightened Christian community, exercised in the grace of giving, there is no system which so nicely meets the want, doing away with all soliciting and subscription committees, and accomplishes the result so efficiently and pleasantly as this very method. To any one who has suffered the unkindnesses attendant upon the circulation of a subscription during long weeks, and even months, of *arduous* toil, it will be a sufficient recommendation of this plan to say that it does away with this necessity.

In addition to the following sample letter, we refer the reader to another specimen under the head of " Pastoral Letter Plan," Chapter V :

DEAR BRETHREN IN CHRIST:

Ten years ago, by the united effort of all the people, we were enabled to erect our present large and prized church edifice. The total cost of the building, when complete and furnished, was $42,496.25. Of this amount, $17,600 was subscribed before awarding the contracts, and $14,250 was added on the day of dedication. Of these amounts, $28,417 was paid in, making a loss of $3.433 on unpaid subscriptions. This left a balance of $14,079.25 unprovided for. The increased expenses and many needed repairs upon the roof have nearly exhausted the annual income of the treasury, and left much of the interest to accumulate, until the entire debt upon the first day of next month will amount to $23,791.67.

It is proposed now to make a final effort to cancel the entire amount, and to aid in accomplishing this most desirable result, you are asked to contribute in a liberal, Christian spirit. In order that you may not, upon the one hand, wrong yourself and family, or upon the other, withhold from God that which is justly his, your pastor desires that you make this matter a subject of earnest prayer for two weeks, and that at the expiration of that time you fill up the accompanying blank and lay it upon the collection plate the following Sabbath. As ye have freely received, so freely give.

First Presbyterian Church,

——— ——— ——— Pa.,

October 12, 1880. 12

The accompanying is the blank to be filled up:

—————— Pa., October 26, 1880.

After prayerfully considering my ability and duty to contribute toward the liquidation of the debt resting upon our church, I will and do hereby cheerfully subscribe the sum of thirteen hundred dollars ($1,300 , to be paid in four quarterly installments, the first to be paid one month from this date.

JOHN STILLWATER.

MONTHLY COLLECTION PLAN.

In a congregation of wealth, we have known $8,000 to be raised in a single year, by setting apart the offerings placed in the collection boxes upon the first Sabbath of each month, for the payment of a church debt.

There are but few congregations in which this plan would accomplish the end to be attained. In its use, great caution would need to be used lest the result should be so meager as to belittle the cause and defeat the success of this, or any plan which might be used subsequently. In most congregations the results of this plan would be disastrous.

MORTGAGE DONATION PLAN.

Where the claims against a congregation are held by people of wealth, or liberality, or both, it occasionally happens that a debt has been canceled by inducing such person, or persons, to surrender their claims.

This may or may not be a good plan, according to circumstances. If the congregation is absolutely so poor as to be unable to pay the debt, or any part of it, then it is a most excellent plan. But if the congregation is merely *unwilling* to pay, or *indifferent* concerning the debt, then such a donation would result injuriously to the temporal as well as the spiritual welfare of the congregation. It is only ruinous to the interests of a congregation to have an individual render it unnecessary for them to put forth any effort. It will enervate, destroy self-respect, and defeat the object of the donor. This is illustrated by the various churches we might enumerate, which have been endowed by a misguided liberality. With no need of raising money to pay a pastor, to aid the poor, or to convert the heathen, they have dragged out a useless existence, until finally they have disbanded, or had a mere nominal existence. Any gift which renders it unnecessary for a congregation to act, is injurious to its best interests. It is better for the congregation to exert itself in raising as much as possible before the balance is donated. This will make the welfare of the church the common interest of all.

Where it is decided to be best for those who hold the mortgages, or notes, to donate the same, and such is the sense of both parties, it is always best to execute such purpose by canceling the claims in a legal

manner, without delay; for life is very uncertain, and
in event of the death of such intended donor, one or
two disinterested heirs are likely to refuse to carry
out the unexecuted purpose of the deceased.

CHURCH-PAPER APPEAL PLAN.

Some congregations rush unadvisedly into debt,
and then seek relief by appeals through the church
papers. As long as the churches continue to withhold
their tithes and free-will offerings from the Lord, so
long will appeals, unless for some very special objects,
continue to be unsuccessful: and as soon as the
churches shall obey God's laws concerning tithes and
offerings, appeals shall cease to seem necessary, for
each congregation in established communities will find
that they have means sufficient. The plan in all ordinary circumstances, is unphilosophical and unsuccessful.

CANVASSING PLAN.

The plan of seeking foreign aid by sending agents
to canvass other congregations is kindred to that of
appeals through the church papers. By all means
avoid both. For an eloquent chapter on the unwill-
ingness of Christians to help their "needy brethren,"
you will only find it necessary to write, asking the
experience of some one who has tried either of these
plans.

THE DEFRAUDING PLAN.

Congregations have been known to borrow money on trustee notes, to give a first, second, and even a third mortgage on the church building and lot, and then in an hour of financial pressure have been known to allow the property to be sold under foreclosure, in order to buy it in at a nominal sum, casting off all the just and legal claims by a single act of villainy. In most instances, the congregations are able to pay the debts, and are guilty of a great crime when they refuse to pay. In other instances they are unable to pay, but are guilty of a crime equally as great, for they have created a debt when there was no possibility of ever paying it.

We might name men who are to-day poor, and dependent upon their daily wages for bread for their families, who have been rendered penniless by similar courses of dishonesty, and, in one or two instances, the transactions seem almost to have been characterized by fraudulent intent. The course of such congregations cannot be too strongly denounced. It will be well when congregations come to recognize the fact that as long as any member of the entire organization has a single dollar's worth of property, he is bound by every sense of right, and every law of God, to use it in paying the debt which he has aided to contract. In the first place, no congregation has a right to create a church debt, but when they do, they become personally responsible, and their individual property, and even their future earnings, are pledged to the payment of that debt, and no injustice which may be practiced under the protection of the civil law can stand justified before God, until this obligation is both acknowledged and discharged. If a body of individuals decide to build a temple, that when completed is given to God in solemn ceremony, any bills which this body of individuals may create, and which remain' unpaid, are most clearly their debts, and not God's at all, nor is it just that God's temple should be sold to pay their debts. God is not in debt, but these individuals are, and that, contrary to God's command, and being their individual debt, their individual property is as justly bound to the payment of this, as it is bound to the payment of any other debt.

An honest congregation cannot take refuge behind the civil law, any more than an honest individual can. Neither can a church debt become " out-lawed." If it ever becomes out-lawed, it can never become out-gospeled. A "church debt," so called, but really the congregation's debt, remains in force as long as the persons live who made it, and they are bound to it by every sense of honor, by every manly principle, and every law of God ; neither can they rid themselves of this obligation by separating themselves from the organization, or removing into the limits of another congregation. The obligation is a personal one, unaffected by time or place, and only relieved by payment or death—and then their estate is justly holding. When people shall come to look at this matter in its true light, they will not be so fast to create " church debts."

CHURCH ENTERTAIMENT PLAN.

After the Church of Rome had preached against the God-ordained law of the tithe, it found itself in the pitiable plight of poverty. To escape from the sad but inevitable consequences of its sin, it sought to replenish its empty coffers by introducing pilgrimages to its thousand shrines, with their bones of saints, sacred relics and pretended miracles. The divine law was supplanted by the sale of indulgences, and giving as an act of worship found its place usurped by lotteries, festivals, shows, theatres and every device by which priestcraft could extort money from a people who knew not the Word of God.

It is only to be lamented that the Protestant Churches have in any measure been given to the use of any of these iniquitous plans for raising money. Too many of our churches which have been dedicated to the glory of God are desecrated by fairs, oyster suppers, dramas, tableaux, lectures, shows, exhibitions and various other things which are ruinous to the financial as well as the spiritual prosperity of the church. Money is not valuable enough to be purchased at so ruinous a price, and the fewer unholy people we gather into the church by these unholy means, the better for the church and for the world.

The process by which a church fair pays church debts is thus described by a Presbyterian elder: "Now, brethren, let us get up a supper and eat ourselves rich. Buy your food. Then give it to the church. Then go buy it back again. Then eat it up, and then—your church debt is paid."

Some time since a young lady inquired by letter of the New York *Tribune* how she could raise some money for a small country church. She writes:

" Do you think it would be advisable to attempt a concert? We have had calico parties, sugar parties, fish ponds, mock post-offices and the like. If you can suggest some new form of entertainment you will earn our sincerest thanks."

To this the *Tribune* answers: "We recommend a revival of religion." This is decidedly the best answer and the best method that could be given. A revival of *genuine* religion so awakens the spirit of benevolence and unites the hearts and efforts of Christians, that all the money needed to carry on the work of the church is freely contributed.

At one of the Christian Conventions, Mr. Moody

was asked : "Are church fairs and sociables wrong ?"

Mr. Moody answered : " Decidedly ! I have not always thought so, but my eyes are open now. It is better to ask direct for money than entice a man to a church fair and make him pay a dollar and a half for an article that cost fifty cents. He goes home and says he has been swindled, but consoles himself with the reflection that he has benefited the church. The idea is that young men go to such entertainments because there are pretty women there. It does no good, and certainly should be discouraged."

" In Scotland it is one of the principles of the United Presbyterian Church not to accept money for sacred uses from unclean hands. As God's agents, or ministers, they decline to take for Him money that, as far as they can see, has not been honestly made.

" When the great Glasgow Bank failure took place some of the directors were members of the United Presbyterian congregations of that city, and one or more of them were large givers—almost the support of their particular churches. When, by the judgment of the civil courts, they were declared to have been guilty of systematic fraud for some years back, their liberal donations were all returned to them, although it more than crippled the congregations who did it."

This was a wisdom which, to most churches, would appear folly, but no surer course could be pursued to

13

secure the divine blessing. If some congregations, such as are almost everywhere to be found, were to refund what they have secured by means of neck-tie parties, exhibitions, oyster suppers and similar devices, they would be robbed of even the little they now seem to have.

We know of no arguments in favor of such entertainments as have been indicated, and some of the arguments against them might be briefly stated as follows :

1. In proportion as they are more frequently used do they despoil the church of its spiritual power.

2. Those who labor faithfully for the success of the enterprise are apt to suffer from unkind speech, or unjust suspicion, in the management of the finances.

3. In most cases they are employed by Christians who withhold from God that which he requires at their hands, while they seek to carry forward the work of the church by drawing the needed funds from " outsiders." They covet the wealth of the wicked, and seek opportunity to gain their influence and money. " Know ye not that the friendship of the world is enmity with God ? Whosoever, therefore, will be a friend of the world is the enemy of God."

4. If not universally, yet quite generally, they alienate from the church some of its most useful members.

5. Whatever other effect these entertainments may

have upon those who are not church members, they surely will not lead poor sinners to the cross of Christ.

6. Those most worldly-minded in the congregation are sure to desire, and apt to succeed, in being at the head of these entertainments, and guard them as best we may, they are almost sure to introduce into them such features as are ruinous to the best interests of the church; a disgusting song spoils the concert, a *double-entendre* the exhibition, cordials, cider and cigars the picnic, a hetrodox statement or irreligious sentiment the lecture—on, and on through the whole list the devil is determined to be in somewhere, or his personal friends will denounce the pastor as an " old fogy," get enraged because they cannot have their own way, dismember the congregation, and then leave in disgust.

7. Last, but by no means the least, of all the evils, is the undeniable fact that church fairs, oyster suppers, and the whole round of church entertainments *are fatal to every impulse and principle of genuine scriptural benevolence.*

GOD'S PLAN.

As God did not design that congregations should ever go into debt in building churches, He gives us no plan for getting them out of debt. The only light which the Bible throws upon this question would have to be gathered from the plans which God has given for securing the means, necessary to erect structures for his worship. The reader is referred to that department in Chapter V.

CAN THE DEBTS UPON THE CHURCHES BE PAID?

Three years ago the recorded loans to the various churches, secured by bond and mortgage, not including loans obtained upon notes and other securities, in the city of New York alone, amounted to the enormous sum of $2,367,886. The various denominations were represented by the following amounts : Presbyterian, $706,000 ; Reformed, $644,000 ; Protestant Episcopal, $453,000 ; Roman Catholic, $229,000 ; Baptist, $212,000 ; Methodist, $79,000 ; Lutheran, $44,886. The debts upon the various churches throughout the United States foot up to such vast millions that when the herculean task of paying them is contemplated, the question naturally arises, Can the debts now resting upon the churches be paid? Let a Christian merchant in his convincing words answer the question :

" That the professed followers of Christ, especially in our day and country, possess a large share of this world's riches, is apparent to the most casual observer. Subject to no persecutions, relieved of the stigma which in the earlier history of the church attached to the Christian name, not liable to be despoiled of their

goods because of their loyalty to their divine Head.
many of those enrolled under the banner of Jesus
rank high as the possessors of material wealth. A
large number of those at the head of our railroad and
canal corporations, our river and ocean steam naviga-
tion companies and shipping firms; many of those
prominent either in the ownership or the management
of our great commercial houses, our telegraph and
insurance companies; not a few of those who have
achieved honorable distinction as financiers, as bank-
ers and brokers, as managers of our savings banks
and trust companies: not a few of those who conduct
on a large scale our lumber, mining, manufacturing,
and agricultural interests, profess allegiance to Him
whose is the earth and the fulness thereof, to whom
belong alike the silver and the gold, and the cattle
upon a thousand hills.

" From those owning broad acres of the richest soil
on which our great staples are grown; from those in
our large cities owning plots of land on which lofty
palaces are reared; from those who manage our great
public works; from engineers, architects, lawyers,
physicians, authors, lecturers, editors, men of letters,
men of science, may be selected many bearing the
Christian name, to whom God has given in greater or
less degree the riches of this world. Scarcely any
honorable secular profession can be named that does

not contribute its quota of those possessed of far more than the mere means of living. In the princely residences of Christians in our cities, their dress, their equipage, their costly entertainments, their general style of living, abundant proof is furnished of the unstinted measure of wealth which God has poured into their lap. In our towns and villages, and in our farming districts, particularly in our seaboard and Middle States, it cannot be gainsaid that Christians share abundantly in the general prosperity of the country.

"The immense, unprecedented sums of money, nearly four hundred and twenty-five millions of dollars, to-day in the savings banks of the two states of New York and Massachusetts, deposited chiefly by the middle and poorer classes, attest the wide distribution of our wealth ; and this extraordinary accumulation has awakened the astonishment and elicited the hearty commendation of keen observers in the Old World. If our religious and benevolent enterprises languish, surely it cannot be for want of means in the hands of the Lord's servants, to whom he has committed the stewardship of wealth."[*]

"That the people of God have an abundance of his money in their hands," says Rev. William Ramsey, "which should be disposed of for the glory of their

[*] J. F. Wyckoff, Esq , in " The Christian Use of Money."

master, no one can doubt. Do they not live, many of
them, in their ceiled palaces, and nearly all of them
in the enjoyments of the comforts of life, and I might
add, of its luxuries, too? Is there a scheme of world-
liness that promises temporal gain; is there a scene
of national joy and amusement not in itself sinful; is
there a new fashion or a new mode invented to make
life more easy; is there a new enterprise to promote
the political prosperity of the nation, or to increase
the glory of our country both at home and abroad; is
there any society founded for the promotion of the
arts, or for the cultivation of letters in this great
nation that does not draw largely upon the treasury
of the Lord through the hands of his people? Point
me to one if you can. Why, then, does the house
of the Lord lie waste, and why are the watchmen on
the walls of Zion faint and dying for the lack of those
means which God's people have directed, in a great
degree, from their appropriate channel? I am not
finding fault with the activity of Christians in any
plan whose tendency is to promote the temporal good
of man. But why should they be active in pushing
forward their researches in science, in the improvement of the arts, in the improvement and refinement
of society in general, and yet leave the *cause of God*
to languish? Does this latter cause promise less
temporal gain? Or does the money thrown into the

treasury of the Lord yield less interest, and less comfort to the body, and less joy and peace to the soul,
than the amount invested in the stocks of earth, that
church members are induced to trust their *thousands*
in the hands of man, while they will not trust their
tens to God for safe keeping? There is something
here radically wrong. If the pride, covetousness, and
selfishness of the church be not the cause of the evil,
do tell me what is."

" Notwithstanding the great debt that presses upon
the church, it could be paid immediately, because the
people of God are able to do it. I speak advisedly,
when I say they are *able* to do it. Look at the
immense wealth that is in this country. Now ask,
into whose hands has God entrusted all this wealth?
You will find that a very large portion of it is in the
hands of those who are the avowed friends and followers of Him who became poor for our sakes. A large
portion of the remainder is held by those who,
although not the professed followers of Christ, are the
decided friends of Christianity—are regular in their
attendance on the means of grace, and are ready to
contribute to the support of every benevolent enterprise. The wealth of this country is not held by the
misanthrope and the foe of the Bible. If the people
of God do not now possess as much of their Lord's
money as is needed to carry forward His work, there

is still enough in the hands of others to do it, which they may obtain. For, as 'the earth is the Lord's, and the fulness thereof,' as ' the wealth of the sinner is laid up for the just,' and as the promise is, ' ask, and ye shall receive,' the amount may be had if the proper means be used. There is money enough, and more than enough, in the hands of Christians to release the houses of their God from the pressure of mortgages and judgment bonds, which now weigh them down. The pewholders in one congregation alone, in this city (Philadelphia), hold property to the amount of, at least, thirty millions of dollars! What a trust is this! And what a fearful responsibility rests upon those who are the stewards of so much of God's money. There are individual Christians among us who hold property from the value of one hundred thousand up to two millions of dollars.

"A gentleman, who certainly has the means of knowing facts like the following, and who is not apt to make groundless statements, recently informed me that the Saviour has entrusted in the hands of one of his people in this city, and which he now holds, more money than has' been received into the treasury of the American Board of Commissioners for Foreign Missions since the year 1812—say, some two and a half or three millions of dollars."

"Now, take what view of this subject you choose, still, I think, you will agree with me in the belief

14

that the people of God have enough of their Lord's money in their hands to pay off al the debt that now rests upon the churches dedicated to his service. The work *can* be done. If the work can be done, it may be asked, why is it not done? I reply, that many Christians have not seriously thought of paying off the debts of their churches; and yet they would cheerfully aid, if any one would lead the way. There may be some who do not wish to do it, and the reason is, they imagine they can make more money for themselves by the operation. I will explain myself. Suppose Mr. A has the sum of $5,000, which he chooses to call his own. He is a member of a church that is in debt $8,000 or $10,000, and is now called on to aid in paying off the debt. He reasons thus: I can give $1,000, and so can others; but as the interest is only *six* per cent., if I keep my thousand dollars, and trade with it, I can make ten, twenty, or even thirty per cent. profit out of it. I will, therefore, cheerfully pay my portion of the interest as it becomes due. I will trade with my Lord's money, and whatever is over the six per cent., which I must pay as my share of the interest money, I will put in my own pocket. And when I am dead the money may go to pay the debt.

"There may be some who feel and act in this way, and it is probable that they think they act wisely. Perhaps they do for this world, but not for the next. Is it the proper course for those to pursue who are the Lord's stewards?"

CHAPTER IV.

HOW TO KEEP CHURCHES OUT OF DEBT.

(ESTABLISHED CHURCHES.)

ADVANCING TOWARD THE TRUE METHOD—THE PEW SYSTEM
—PEW RENTING—ARGUMENTS IN FAVOR OF—AGAINST—
MODES OF RENTING PEWS—AT AUCTION—FROM SCHED-
ULE—SITTINGS FOR THE POOR—RENTAL AGREEMENTS—
NOTICES—COLLECTING PEW RENTS—PAYMENT IN ENVE-
LOPES—PROVIDING FOR DEFICIENCIES—TAX UPON PEWS
OWNED BY ATTENDANTS—THE FREE PEW SYSTEM—VOL-
UNTARY CONTRIBUTIONS — ANNUAL SUBSCRIPTIONS —
ORIGIN AND DEFECTS—PERMANENT SUBSCRIPTION CON-
SIDERED—FORMS OF NOTICES—THE ENVELOPE SYSTEM—
EXCELLENCIES OF — HOW INTRODUCED — SECURING
PLEDGES — FORMS OF—A SYSTEM UNITING THE LOCAL
AND FOREIGN WORK—THE BELLEFONTE METHOD—
FORMS OF ENVELOPES—THE TREASURER'S BOOK—BILLS
AND REMINDERS—THE SCRIPTURAL METHOD—CONCLU-
SION.

All over this country thousands of churches are
annually failing to pay current expenses, ministers
are perplexed, people are disheartened, and the church
of Christ is hindered in its great work of saving souls.
This is a natural result of the sin of departing from
God's ordained method of sustaining His cause upon
earth; and not until the Christian church shall fully
recognize the divine law of the tithe, can we ever

intelligently hope for a removal of the great curses
which impede the church's progress.

During the past decade of years, advances have
been made toward the true scriptural method of supporting the church. This introduction of the *better*,
is the gradual but sure preparation of the church for
the eventual return to the *best ;* and in presenting the
following methods, now in use by the various congregations, we do so hoping that none will rest satisfied
with the improvement of their present system, or the
introduction of something better, or be satisfied with
any improvement, only as it indicates progress and
becomes a promise of the final acceptance, by the people, of that which is God's own method.

THE PEW SYSTEM.

Seats in churches are a somewhat modern convenience, nor are they even now in use in most Roman
Catholic countries. Among those earliest mentioned
we find them in the churches of the Normans, made of
stone, and projecting from the walls around the whole
interior, except the east side. In the fourteenth century low wooden seats were promiscuously placed
about the floor, with the privilege of personal claim
to any one particular seat granted only to noblemen.
About the middle of the sixteenth century seats were
more fully provided and more regularly placed, the
entrance being guarded by crossbars engraved with

the initials of the occupant, but just when the custom of renting pews was first introduced might be difficult accurately to ascertain.

PEW RENTING.

While there is much which may be truthfully and forcibly said against the system of raising the money necessary to meet the current expenses of the church by the renting of pews, yet there are some things to be said in its favor. While many, from a mere desire to offer some excuse for not attending church, will object to going where the seats are rented, there are but few with whom this is the *real* cause of their absence from the house of God. Where there is one of the honest few detained on this account, there will be two, or more, of another class, who have rented a pew, because they desire recognition in some church society, and who, from Sunday to Sunday, are found in their pews, not so much from a love of church going, as a feeling, when Sunday morning comes—" Well, I pay for a seat, and I guess I might as well go and occupy it." And some day, when actuated by no higher motive, a truth thus dropped by the " wayside " may result in the salvation of a soul and the addition to the church of a useful member.

Another advantage of the pew system is that it enables entire families to worship God together. It secures for each family their own particular seat, and when once the entire congregation is assembled, the pastor, by scanning the audience, can readily tell who of his regular attendants are absent, and when missed from their regular places a second time, inquiry may be made and the cause of absence ascertained.

Then again, there are many persons who contribute liberally of their time and money to secure a church home for themselves, and in that church they have a local attachment for some particular pew. They object to having disinterested parties placed upon equal footing and helped to the most desirable sittings. They desire, when starting for church, to know that they are to find comfortable seats, not being left to the alternatives of going long before the hour of service, or be crowded into some uncomfortable quarter of the church. Regular attendents much prefer some regular sitting.

Perhaps the strongest argument urged by the advocates of this system is that its success has gained for it a quite general acceptance. Rev. E. N. White, D. D., of New York, says concerning the system of renting pews:

" In practice this plan has proved financially the best that has yet been devised. It certainly may be so managed that no invidious class distinctions shall be made, and so that no one need be repelled from the church by inability to pay. The differences in price, or even in location of sittings, do not necessarily trench upon the perfect brotherhood and true equality of fellow-Christians worshiping together. No honest man who fears God and pays his debts finds his self-respect touched because his house is smaller or his clothes coarser than his neighbor's; nor is he less respected by any neighbor whose respect is worth having. Why, then, in the house of God need jealousy and heart-burning follow upon differences in money-ability? We often hear the charge made that the poor are kept away from our churches, but it would be hard to find, even in this money-loving city, a church where a true Christian is shut out on account of poverty, or where, because of humble attire or smallness of contribution, he is treated with disrespect.

"It may be said that under a judicious system of pew-rentals a church without a debt and without dissension, in any town where it is surrounded by a stable and well-to-do population, has before it a very simple problem, financially. It can hardly fail of a regular and sufficient income; and to be successful financially it has only to keep its expenses within its income."

AGAINST PEW RENTING.

Some of the chief arguments urged against the renting of pews are :

1. That it leads to a disparagement of the very class of persons who are the special objects of divine regard. It makes money the standard of worth, causing the congregation to say to the rich, " sit thou here in a good place," and to the poor, " stand thou here, or sit here under my footstool."

2. That it *tends* to exclude strangers and such as are not regular pewholders.

3. That it educates people to be parsimonious and mean, causing them to do such disreputable things as rent a *half* pew, and then occupy a *whole* one.

4. That it is not only not authorized by, but is inconsistent with the principles of the gospel.

5. That it despoils giving for the support and spread of the gospel of all its value as an act of worship, converting this essential portion of divine service into an impost levied upon the other portions of the service of God. While this result does not of necessity attach itself to the system, yet all who have had much to do with the renting of pews will have been convinced that many, if not most persons enter into the contract from a purely business standpoint, driving as sharp a bargain in the church as in the world. The time is coming, when "giving" for the support of the support of the gospel, both at home and abroad, shall again be regarded in the light of God's word. When the amount shall be increased to the proportion of a

tithe, and the giving or paying of it shall not only be a part of the worship of the sanctuary, but an essential, an indisputable portion.

MODES OF RENTING PEWS.

One quite common method of renting pews is by fixing a special day, and after giving due notice, have all desiring to become pewholders assemble at the specified time, and then rent the pews according to one of two plans, viz :

At Auction.—The pews are frequently set up at auction, and struck off for one year to the highest bidder. In this way a large amount of money is sometimes secured by the rental of the choice pews, but unless the preacher is exceedingly popular, or some other unusual excitant quickens a vehement competition until all the pews are sold, the entire amount will fall short of that which might be realized by some other method.

Some congregations fix a graded schedule of prices, accepting no bid which falls below this, they sell to the highest bidder. This plan protects the pews from being rented at less than the apprizal rates. Others, again, attach a fixed value to each pew, and then sell at auction, not the pew, but the *choice*, or privilege of making first and succeeding choice of all the pews. The bid is for the choice, to which the regular rental price of the pew is added. The following are the con-

15

ditions of sale, published by a large congregation in Brooklyn, N. Y.:

" Each pew has a fixed valuation, and *the choice* of all in the house is offered, without reservation for previous occupants, to the highest bidder.

" Each aisle seat has a fixed valuation, and is offered to the highest bidder for a premium above that valuation. The seats are known by the same numbers as the pews to which they are attached.

" Payment of rent for pews is required semi-annually in advance, and for aisle seats the whole year in advance.

" The trustees reserve, and will exercise, the right to re let any pew or seat, *oa account of the original lessee*, if the rent is not paid within thirty days after becoming due.

" No bid will be accepted from those in arrears.

" No pew, or part of a pew, nor any aisle seat, will be rented either at the public renting or at any time thereafter, for a less period than until January next.

" The pews and seats are rented with the understanding that if not occupied at least ten minutes before the commencement of the services, they may then be assigned to strangers.

" All regular attendants at the church are expected to rent sittings, in order that the large current expenses may be shared by the whole congregation.

" The house will be open every morning in January, after the public renting, from 8 to 9 o'clock, and on Saturday evenings from 7 to 9 o'clock ; and a person will be in attendance to rent such pews and seats as remain undisposed of, and to receive payments of rent.   BY ORDER OF THE TRUSTEES."

The sale of pews by public auction tends to excite among the members a spirit of rivalry, jealousy, personal pride and vain glory, and may be conducted in such a manner as to subvert the very cause Christ had in view in establishing His church upon the earth.

Public Rental, not at Auction.—The custom of renting pews at auction lacks the approval of God's Word, and of many Christians whose judgment is worthy of great respect. Most congregations renting pews announce the day and hour, have a graded schedule of prices, and rent, not to the highest bidder, but to such as first notify the committee of their choice. The schedule of valuation, if judiciously arranged, may serve an excellent purpose in fixing the income of the church so that is shall fully meet the annual expenditures, and also avoid great diversity in the prices of pews equally desirable. If the pews are all rented each successive year, the former occupants are usually granted the first refusal.

A more desirable method is to rent the pews for an *indefinite* period, at a fixed rate, to be paid monthly,

quarterly, semi-annually, or annually, in advance.
The lessee may at any time vacate the pew by giving
notice of the same in writing, and paying all arrearages.
At least twice a year public attention should be called
to the matter, and new attendants given an opportunity to secure regular seats ; or this matter may be
left in the hands of a judicious committee, who shall
personally call upon all such as should be pewholders.

One difficulty often arises in churches where seats
are rented. There are frequently those who are too
proud to sit anywhere except in the very best pews
the church affords, and are, at the same time, too
mean or too poor to pay the price which the sitting
will and should reasonably bring. As another says,
they are frequently " of that cl. ss who can pay freely
for tickets to the theatre, or other places of popular
amusement ; can hire a carriage for a Sunday drive to
the park ; can entertain company splendidly at Sunday dinners "— and in short who can pay for anything
except religion. They are not willing to sacrifice
their pride to the best interests of the church, but
want the church and all its interests sacrificed to their
personal vain glory. The fewer of this class of people you have in your church the better, for when the
church has to be sacrificed to satisfy the pride of
individuals, its usefulness is at an end. Such people
have not, and cannot have the best interests of the

church at heart, and the sooner they seek sittings somewhere else, the better for your church, at least.

SITTINGS FOR THE POOR.

God has decreed that "The poor shall never cease out of the land" (Deut. xv: 11 . In every age they are to be a living illustration, to the church, of the condition to which the King of kings condescended for the salvation alike of rich and poor. They are not to be slighted or neglected by the church founded by Him, who for our sakes became poor. They should be made as welcome, and treated as cordially in our churches, as those who are rich in this world's goods. If by overt act, or cold neglect they be excluded, Christ may say to such church in that day, inasmuch as ye have shown this disrespect unto one of the least of these, my brethren, ye have shown it unto me.

Sittings, or pews, may be secured for the poor in several ways :

1. Every third or fourth pew may be left for occupancy by the poor, or they may by assigned to particular families.

2. The pews on one side of each of the aisles may be reserved for the poor and strangers. If visitors should be sufficiently numerous, any invidious distinctions on account of poverty would be overcome.

3. Encouraging those who are able, to hire one or more pews to be occupied by the poor.

4. Seats may be assigned by the committee to all such as shall apply after being cordially invited.

5. Inducing the more wealthy to contribute to the formation of a fund, from which shall be paid all arrearages accumulating on the pews occupied by such as are really unable to pay in full the regular rental. If judiciously managed, this may aid in doing away with all humiliating distinctions.

6. If the income of the church is sufficient to permit, the poor may be allowed, with reasonable restrictions, to rent pews at the schedule rates, with the understanding that what they lack, after making an honest effort to pay, should be cancelled by the sanction of the official board of the church. This action to take place at stated intervals, not exceeding one year.

7. By an honest and hearty spirit of cordiality upon the part of the entire congregation, making both rich and poor feel thoroughly at home in *their* pews; or, as another aptly expresses it: " It is hoped that such a spirit will prevail, that each member will be willing to pay the highest price he is able, and that, too, for the poorest sitting in the house; and then be ready to give that up every Sunday to strangers, or, which is better, to fill it with sinners whom he shall bring in, while he himself sits in the aisle or on a chair in the corner. This is the principle of sacrifice which lies at

the foundation of our religion. 'Christ pleased not Himself.' Neither should we. We *must* have the spirit of Christ, else we are none of His. The church can make rapid progress upon no other principle."

Other ways may suggest themselves. In a large and wealthy congregation in the state of New York, in remodeling their church, to avoid the crowding of the poor into the gallery, or in some corner of the church, the seats were removed from the gallery, the space laid off into compartments, carpeted, supplied with comfortable chairs, and rented at a high price by the more wealthy, in order to allow more space for the poor and strangers, who were furnished some of the best sittings in the church. This, and like efforts, are commendable.

SEAT RENTAL AGREEMENTS.

Where seats are rented there are usually found such as are glad to escape the payment of the same by the use of any and every unprincipled pretext. At the end of each quarter the collector is evaded, or some fault is found with the minister, the church wardens, or some body, or some thing, until finally the year is past and the rent remains unpaid. Frequently this class of people occupy some of the choicest sittings— sittings which could easily be rented to good and re- sponsible parties, if this dishonest class could only be gotten rid of. To meet this class of persons the

author, in his first charge, found it necessary to devise
some plan which would make fruitless excuses, such
as : "When some of the men who are officers in the
church shall pay me what they owe me, then I will
pay the church." "The members of the church have
wronged and injured me and I don't intend to contribute to the support of such an organization." "The
party sitting just in front of me has a more desirable
pew, and yet pays less rent than you ask of me. If
this is the unequal and unfair way the church is to be
run, I do not propose to pay another cent." To meet
these and a multitude of other excuses equally as
sensible (!) agreements printed as the sample given
below, and bound in cheap form, served an excellent
purpose:

Zion's Evangelical Lutheran Church.
————— N. Y.,   188

*I hereby agree to take seat No.   for one
year from   18   , at an
annual rental of $, to be paid to the Treas-
urer in quarterly installments at the end of each quarter, and if not paid in fifteen days after the date upon
which it falls due, I then agree to pay 5 per cent. additional to the collector.*

These agreements tend to secure prompt payments.
There can be no disputing the fact that the parties

really rented a pew. Neither can they dispute the price, nor the length of time agreed upon. It secures the church against financial loss by parties removing during the year. To save the five per cent., few will allow the fifteen days to expire, and the treasurer or collector will be spared much unpleasant work in going around making collections. These and other advantages attend its use.

The fear that any would refuse to sign it will prove groundless, if the leading members of the church will but set the example, and then make no exception to the rule. We have never known any one to refuse to sign the agreements, and when once signed, the petty excuses were no longer encountered, but all paid promptly, and the church lost no more money by bad debts of this sort.

PEW-RENT NOTICES.

There are many persons who are sensitive about receiving a pew-rent notice, but church business must be done in a business-like manner. It should, therefore, be announced that at regular intervals notices will be mailed to each and every person indebted to the church. Should there be any who object to receiving such notice, they may easily avoid the same by paying in advance.

The following may suggest a form of pew-rent notice:

16

Carthage, Ill.   188

M

To FIRST LUTHERAN CHURCH, Dr.

To pew rent from   188 *to*   188 $

After fifteen days from date, 5 per cent will be added for collection.

Treasurer.

COLLECTING PEW RENTS.

As a rule it is almost universally best to have the pew rents paid either monthly, or quarterly, *in advance.* Those who fail to call on the treasurer of the church and pay punctually, should be called upon promptly If much time is permitted to elapse, it tends to cultivate a spirit of neglect upon the part of all pewholders, and disastrous results are sure to follow. This will take time, but is worthy of even more time and inconvenience than it costs. The interests of the church should be committed into the hands of *only such* as are willing to devote to it *all* the time and attention it demands.

One of the churches of a city in Pennsylvania was continually annoyed with annual deficits. Expenses could not be met, the pastor could not be paid promptly, together with all the other evils which follow in the train. The trouble was that the finances simply lacked personal supervision, and that prudent management needed to render any extensive enterprise a success. The entire financial affairs of the church were finally entrusted to a competent lady, who would devote the necessary time to the work. The congregation was canvassed, and a larger number of pews were rented as a result. Once a month the church bell was rung to notify all that the monthly installments were due, and that the treasurer would be in the church half a day to receive the same. The result need not be told. Now the income exceeds the expenditures, the pastor is paid promptly, no bill need be presented twice, money always in the treasury, everything moving along pleasantly, and increased usefulness comes as the attendant result. The financial evil in many churches might easily be cured simply by securing one who is willing to devote the time required by the work.

PAYMENT IN ENVELOPES.

In a few churches envelopes are used for the payment of pew rents. It saves the treasurer much trouble, and the pewholder much annoyance. The idea is capital. There is but one question, however, and that is this: Is it right to pay accounts on the Lord's Day? According to the secular view held by many concerning the support of the church, it would, most assuredly, be as wrong to pay pew rent on Sunday as to pay your grocer or butcher. But where giving for the support of the gospel at home is understood by the people to be as much an act of worship as giving for the spread of the gospel and the conversion of the heathen, then it becomes not only admissable, but a positive good, an enjoined duty. Let us bring back the offertory into our churches, and restore giving to its usurped place in worship.

But the mere fact that the pews are rented is likely to be regarded as *prima facie* evidence of the predominance of the purely commercial idea in the management of the finances of the church, and this would render the payment of pew rents upon the Sabbath, to say the least, a very questionable procedure.

We annex a single, but good, specimen of the envelopes used :

By the rules of the church and congregation, all pew rents are payable monthly, in advance.

Calvary Baptist Church.

From

For rent of   *Pew No.*

For   , 188 . $

☞ Please enclose in this envelope the amount due, and place it in one of the boxes near the door, or hand it to the treasurer, the first Sunday in the month.

TO PROVIDE FOR DEFICIENCIES.

Should the amount realized from the rent of the pews be insufficient to meet current expenses, such deficiencies should always be provided for at the beginning of the year. This might be done by :

1. Having the officers of the church make a liberal estimate for the ensuing year. It should include everything necessary—salaries, insurance, interest, repairs and all incidental expenses, including also shrinkage and other contingencies.

2. Make a fair estimate of the regular income from pews, collections, &c., and by deducting this from the former, all may see at once the amount still to be provided for.

3. Let this be *apportioned* among the regular attendants. It is usually best to appoint a goodly number on the apportionment committee, as it tends to help all who " feel poor " to see that they are even more able to give than others whose circumstances they have misjudged.

4. Each individual should then be notified of the amount which the committee had hoped he might be able to give, and asked to satisfy the same.

Such amounts might be paid in weekly, monthly, or quarterly installments, *in advance*, by the use of envelopes, or regular collectors might be sent to make regular collections.

TAX UPON PEWS OWNED BY ATTENDANTS.

Where churches have been built upon the joint-ownership plan, it is usually necessary to provide for the current expenses of the church by levying an annual tax upon pews owned by attendants, and supplementing this by renting all unsold pews. The system is fraught with complications and would probably never have been originated had it not been for the influence of the individual proprietorship argument in inducing parties to subscribe more liberally to the building fund.

Its disadvantages may be stated in part as :

1. It leads to an inequality in the amounts paid by the two classes—those who own, and those who rent pews.

2. The trustees are likely to be perplexed in the disposition of such pews as are owned by non-residents.

3. It tends to cause those who are simply the lessees to feel but a partial interest in both the temporal and spiritual affairs of the church. See this subject more fully treated in the succeeding chapter under the "Joint Ownership" plan.

THE FREE PEW SYSTEM.

The system of having all the pews free is, unquestionably, the true system. It is the only custom which is accordant with the principles of the Biblical method of church support, and the one which must again become universal when the duty of giving *at least* one-tenth for the direct support of the church, aside from new enterprises which are to be provided for by *free-will* offerings and the support of the poor by *alms-giving*—I say, when these principles shall again be preached and the people understand their duty in this matter, then will the free pew system again become universal. Many of the methods by which money is now secured for church support are simply human devices which appeal more to personal pride, a spirit of emulation, business interests and other unscriptural motives, rather than to a sense of obligation as stewards to comply with the require-ments of God, the great proprietor of all things.

But before coming to the scriptural method for pro-viding for the annual expenses of the church, there are several other methods in use which properly come under the head of the free church, or free pew system, which are worthy of presentation.

VOLUNTARY CONTRIBUTIONS.

Many churches which are using a sort of "give what you please, or as little as you please" system, try to dignify the same by the scriptural title of " Free-Will Offerings." This is a misnomer, a per-version, a degrading of the term from its Biblical meaning. What free-will offerings were, and still are, will be shown later in its proper place. Even the other term, " voluntary contributions," is, or at least may be, according to circumstances, susceptible of grave misapprehensions, and we use it simply to designate the system which is known by that name.

In speaking of the voluntary contribution plan, the pastor of a church in New York city says: "In a general way, it may be said that the *ideal* church would be absolutely a *free* church.

"Built by a *free* subscription and dedicated free from debt, it would provide for its expenses by free-will offerings, brought as an act of worship, at each service. Each member would give each week as the Lord prospered him: no man would know the amount of another's gift; it would be a sacred confidence between the giver and his Divine Master.

"This ideal method could be successful, practically, if the Millennium had dawned, and all Christians were absolutely conscientious and truly devoted to their Lord. In practice, men left thus entirely to the dominion of conscience fail as signally in this duty as in every other. It is more interesting from a psychological than a religious point of view to notice how many Christians there are who seem to care very little that the Lord knows how stingy they are, if it is reasonably sure that no one else knows it.

"When I was in Paris, twenty years ago, the Sunday collections of the American congregation, then worshiping in a hired chapel, were gathered in a *hat*. Some shrewd Yankee suggested that it would pay to buy open *plates*. It was done. It was reported that immediately the contributions were nearly doubled. No one meant to be mean; but there is an unconscious, involuntary, almost automatic connection between the publicity and the amount of a contribution.

"If such ideal plan for supporting a church has ever been tried, the career of that church has been so brief that it has left no history."

Here is just where the term "voluntary," as applied to this system, is vague and indefinite. All giving of tithes, free-will offerings and alms is and ever has been voluntary, the same as all moral action.

If the author of the above means that a congregation composed of persons who have no knowledge of what amount it is their duty to give, and are left to contribute as little as selfishness may suggest, will not, under these circumstances, give sufficient to support a church, then his last statement is true—true to the very letter. But if he means that Christians left to the dominion of an *enlightened* conscience will not contribute alike religiously and liberally, then his statement tends to mislead, as it is not in accordance with facts. Without much mental effort we might name at least several congregations where the duty of giving is faithfully preached, where all the contributions are strictly voluntary, and where the amount is

17

left for each contributor to determine in the fear of
God, with a knowledge of the fact that no human
being shall know whether the contribution be much or
little.   Personal pride, public display, a spirit of
emulation, business interest—none of these have any
influence upon the congregation, and yet the annual
contributions aggregate thousands of dollars.   Let a
single instance suffice:

The New York *Observer*, in noticing the valedictory
services of Rev. J. D. Bruen, pastor of the Presbyterian church, at Summit, N. J., gives the following account of the congregation: "Mr. Bruen is the first
pastor, and came to the church in 1871.   It was just
organized with nineteen members, and was without
property.   Seven years and a half have passed.   The
parish has now a beautiful church building and parsonage, and the church has received into her membership 102 by certificate and 101 by profession of faith.
In all, 203 members added to the original 19 in eight
years.   Remarkable as this work has been, yet the
most remarkable thing about the church is its financial system, or rather lack of system.   They used no
envelopes, had no pew rents, said nothing about money
matters, and left it to every man's conscience to keep
him to his duty.   The plate was passed morning and
evening, and by this means they received over $18,000
a year.   We do not like the plan, but we cannot help

confessing that its marvelous success in these most trying times shows conclusively that more depends on conscience, and less on envelopes than we had thought, at least in congregations like that at Summit, composed largely of people of education."

In a general way concerning the " voluntary contribution " system, it may be said, that, if introduced where no due sense of obligation to the divine command already exists, and where the duty is not clearly, frequently and faithfully preached, it will become one of the most unbusiness-like, unscriptural and unsuccessful of all plans. But, on the other hand, if accompanied by a faithful presentation and clear understanding of the divine requirements, it may then approach, or even attain, to the scriptural standard. It is capable of rendering the church, or its ministers, either princes or paupers. A Presbyterian pastor says of it :

" It is a plan that will not run itself. It must be constantly pushed, and always kept before the congregation. It is a little apt to weary in the end. It has often proved successful when managed by a pastor or officer who is an enthusiast in regard to it; but as often it has signally failed. As a matter of fact, the history of ' free churches ' in this city (New York) has been disastrous. Among Presbyterians they have always failed."

But few congregations have been sufficiently instructed to use this plan successfully without considerable machinery, and therefore the envelope system, with its various modifications, has been much more successful.

ANNUAL SUBSCRIPTION.

There still are a goodly number of congregations in rural districts and new fields, which seek to provide for the support of a pastor and current expenses by circulating a subscription at the end of each year. This method, or want of method, is doubtless an outgrowth of the early years when many congregations sought to supplement the amount received from mission boards by circulating a subscription each fall, which was about the only time in all the year when new settlers had any ready money, and would consequently prefer to pay then for the entire year. But while the occasion which begat it has passed away, still the horrid practice, after having outlived its usefulness, continues to hobble along the decades, yea, and even centuries.

If there is a single thing that can be said in favor of this plan, we confess to not knowing what it is, unless it be that the little which is accomplished by means of it is better than nothing at all.

There is much which may be said against the annual subscription plan:

1. It almost universally fails to provide the necessary amount, and leads to questionable methods for securing the deficiency.

2. It leaves the church or its officers to struggle each year, and all the time, with accruing obligations.

3. It annually tempts all who have become estranged from the pastor to withhold their support and to use their influence to defeat the success of the measure, in order to "starve the minister out."

4. It induces people to seek occasion to find all manner of fault, in order to avoid the payment of a just, or equitable amount.

5. It asks in a single payment for an amount, which, if paid in weekly installments, would seem insignificant, but when asked at the end of the year seems startling. Many who could not pay $5 at any one time could readily pay ten cents a week, and others who would be able to pay $50 in weekly installments would not think of giving the whole amount in a single payment.

6. It is unscriptural, unphilosophical and unsuccessful.

PERMANENT SUBSCRIPTION.

The permanent subscription does not of necessity suffer all the disadvantages of the annual subscription. If it does not leave the time and mode of payment optional with each subscriber, but affords some

reliable guarantee that the money will be forthcoming
in due time to meet the demands of the cause, then it
may, with judicious management, attain a more
worthy rank among other methods. It is permanent
only in that it requires no annual renewals. Changes
are from time to time to be made in the amounts.
Each year will witness commercial changes. Some of
moderate means will grow wealthy, while sickness or
financial reverses will render others less able to contribute. "Paul says (2 Cor., viii., 13, 14 . that he
will not have one eased and another burdened in these
matters, but that there be an *equality*—he means a
proportionate equality. Men of large property in the
church, who wish to obey the Word of God, do well
to remember that a contribution of $500 from a man
worth $500,000 is far less burdensome than one of $5
from a widow whose entire estate would not bring
$500. Nevertheless, the widow should give her
share. And where any member seems to be falling
below his proportionate equality in bearing the church
expenses, the church should, in a kind and fraternal
spirit, call his attention to the subject."

Because the subscription bears the name of "permanent," it is liable to be neglected or forgotten. This
should not be the case, but at least twice each year it
should be examined with a view to increase and additions.

As the subscription does not require annual renewal, the time and labor heretofore expended in soliciting funds, year by year, may be turned into other channels, the only work needed being for the filling of vacancies as they occur.

It is always best to make a full estimate of all the probable expenses of the church for the ensuing year, allowing a liberal amount for contingent expenses, and then before starting the committee to secure subscriptions, it is better to apportion the entire amount among all members and attendants. Each member of every family, even to the small children, should be invited to subscribe something. In this way the amount will not only be greatly increased, but all will be exercised in this means of grace, and those who are soon to occupy the places of their seniors in the church will be accustomed to contribute, and future years will reveal the beneficent results of this method. By all means have the children contribute something. This, however, must be done in such a way as to augment the amounts subscribed by the older members of the family, or the church will fall into the pitiable plight of being entirely dependent upon the children or the Sunday-school. The church should support the Sunday-school, and not the Sunday-school the church.

If the results of the subscription are not sufficient

to meet the estimated expenditure, it is doubtless best to renew the effort *at once ;* or by general consent, secured at first, or subsequently, add to the amounts already subscribed such a uniform percentage as the circumstances may require. This would let the balance fall equally upon all.

Each subscription is to remain in force until some specified officer of the church shall have been notified in writing by any seeking release from the amount subscribed. This is essential, or the church will be left with arrearages by the failure of parties to pay the amount the church had a right to expect.

Collections should be faithfully and regularly made. Notices should be sent monthly to those in arrears. These may be of various forms. The following is a sample :

———————*N. Y., Dec.* 16, 1880.

M......

To the *FIRST LUTHERAN CHURCH*, Dr.

To amount of subscription for support of
worship, beginning April 1, 1880........$
Cr. By amount paid...................$
Amount now due..... ....$

Please pay to the Treasurer at your earliest convenience.

Or, if thought preferable, the congregation may be divided into several districts, each of these having a collector, who shall keep the accounts of all subscribers residing in his district, and each of the collectors shall render a regular monthly statement, *in writing*, to the treasurer. Care must always be exercised in the selection of collectors, and all must understand that the money is to be paid to the treasurer promptly. The treasurer should also render a quarterly statement to the vestry of the church ; this may be simply a written statement of amounts received and disbursed, or it may be an itemized account. Let the money of the church be guarded, so as to protect the character of the collectors and treasurer, and this will at the same time protect the church. A clear and explicit statement should be rendered annually to the congregation ; this should be printed and freely distributed. It will more than pay the expense, in the rich return of confidence.

This method may be made :

1. To provide for the expenses of the church at the beginning of the year.

2. To conveniently furnish the money to meet all bills as they become due.

3. To do away with the necessity of continual, or repeated begging at the stated services of the Sabbath.

4. It may also be made to supersede the necessity of oyster suppers, festivals, dramatic exhibitions and the like, which, defend them as best we may, are of

18

questionable tendencies, and attended with damaging results.

5. This method may be made to lead the way to the introduction of the envelope system, and the giving of the scriptural tithe.

THE ENVELOPE SYSTEM.

During the past decade, the old system of pew rentals has been largely superseded by a system of regular offerings, placed in envelopes, and at short and regular intervals deposited in the collection basket at the stated times of divine worship. The system has met with unrivalled success because of its flexibility, accommodating itself to the diversified wants of the various congregations. It admits of adjustment to a system of quarterly, monthly or weekly payments in different churches, or is suited to accommodate all these classes in a single congregation. It is simple, easily understood by all, and may be rendered effective either with much or little machinery. It is easily introduced, and meets with more hearty approval from year to year. In addition, it has been more successful in securing the amounts necessary to provide for the support of the gospel, at home and abroad, than any other system in use since the apostate church of Rome, three centuries before the Ref. rmation, substituted the unscriptural theory of " Competent Maintenance " for the heaven-ordained law of the " Divine Right of the Tithe."

Besides these, the envelope system, properly worked,

1. Is well suited to reach *every* member.

2. It secures the small gifts, keeping open the rills which enlarge the stream of Christian beneficence. It has the correct principle of " small gifts from many givers, at regular and frequent intervals."

3. Because of its frequency, it enjoys the advantages of moral discipline, and serves an excellent purpose in abating the force of avarice—" take heed, and beware of covetousness."

4. It elevates giving to its proper place as a part of divine worship.

5. It makes ability the standard of duty.

6. It leads each member of the church to give systematically, as well as introduces method and system into the finances of the church.

7. The first beneficent result of the system was, that it secured " more giving;" but the gradual and exalted tendencies are to secure " giving more." It seems to us to be the forerunner of the church's return to the scriptural standard of giving at least a tithe for the support and spread of the gospel.

The success of the envelope system renders it unnecessary to defend it against the charges of being unserviceable, mechanical, childish, or complicated. Its continued success and increasing usefulness give clear testimony in its defense.

It remains simply to give a *few* plans, such as may prove suggestive in aiding some to perfect a plan already in use, or may aid others in introducing the system which has secured such desirable results elsewhere.

It might be best for us to remind all that the success of this, or any plan, is in its being thoroughly worked. Some strong hand and earnest heart must be at the wheel, guiding to a successful issue the interests of each congregation, or the finances of the church, like an unguided vessel, will float in the thousand directions of shipwreck, and lose the one safe and only course which leads to port. A poor plan well worked is better than the best plan poorly worked. " The first condition of success is the unequivocal influence of the pastor in favor of some plan of systematic giving. The pastor must devise a plan, must present it, must advocate it, must get the sanction of his church for it, must preach to the people about it, and must pray publicly for God's blessing upon it."

It would be impracticable to lay down arbitrary rules. What will answer in one congregation or community would prove a failure in another, but general principles along with a variety of methods will greatly aid in securing a more universal usefulness among the different congregations.

An Estimate.—The first step in the introduction of the envelope system is to make an estimate of the entire amount necessary to meet all the expenses of the ensuing year. This should include : 1. Pastor's salary. 2. Rent of parsonage. 3. Furniture of parsonage. 4. For aiding the sick and poor. 5. For sacramental purposes. 6. Presiding Elder's allowance. 7. Assessment for the Bishops. 8 Sexton. 9. Fuel and lights. 10. Water rent. 11. Insurance. 12. Interest on debt. 13. Reduction of debt. 14. Repairs. 15. Incidentals. 16. A percentage for unpaid pledges. 17. Sunday-school work. 18. Support of local missions. 19. Taxes. 20. Synodical assessments (not for missions, &c) 21. Any and all other expenses to be provided for. These various amounts added, will give the sum necessary for the work of the year.

Securing Pledges.—The officers of the church, or some judiciously selected committee, may apportion this amount so as to rest equitably upon all members and supporters of the church, and then secure the pledges by dividing the congregation into districts, and appointing judicious persons to canvass the same. Or a more successful method is to send a circular letter to each supporter of the church. The following, taken from "*Helps to Official Members,*" by Rev. James Porter, D. D., may prove suggestive :

Dear Sir: The committee appointed to apportion the amount necessary for the support of the ——— Methodist Episcopal Church for the present year among its members and the congregation, have concluded, after due deliberation, that you can afford, and will be willing to pay the sum of ——— dollars. If you acquiesce in this conclusion, you will please to pay the same in monthly installments, inclosing the amount in an envelope, writing your name, with the amount inclosed, upon the outside, and depositing the same in the basket or box on the first Sabbath in each month, when it will be passed around in the church to receive these monthly payments. If you demur at the apportionment, you will please inform A. B., our treasurer, immediately, stating to him what amount you will pay in the manner aforesaid.

Yours truly, for the committee,

C. D., Secretary.

The pledges may be secured without the apportionment plan by circulating cards, or circular letters, something like the following:

Please deposit this card in the basket with your first envelope.

I HEREBY AGREE to contribute
WEEKLY,

for the support of the Church with which I have the privilege of being associated.

188

"Upon the first day of the week let every one of you lay by him in store as God hath prospered him."—1 Cor. xvi. 2.

The "Church of the Strangers" depends upon the voluntary donations and the subscriptions of its friends and members.

I promise to pay to the Treasurer of the "CHURCH OF THE STRANGERS" the amount stated below, per week, until I otherwise direct.

Name

P. O. Address

Weekly Subscriptions, $ *Cts.*

Date, 1st of

WHEN FILLED, RETURN TO F. A. CRANE, 257 BROADWAY, N. Y.

"God loveth a cheerful giver."—2 Cor. ix. 7.

"He which soweth bountifully shall reap also bountifully."—2 Cor. x. 6.

"So hath the Lord ordained, that they which preach the gospel shall live of the gospel."—1 Cor. ix 14.

"Honor the Lord with thy substance." "To do good, and to communicate, forget not." "God loveth a cheerful giver." "Give, and it shall be given unto you." "Upon the first day of the week......as God hath prospered him."

Ninth Street Baptist Church.

FOR SUPPORT OF WORSHIP.

Beginning April 1, 188 .

I will give ...   per week, for one year, to the object named above.

Name

Residence

The above subscription will be taken up each SABBATH MORNING. Envelopes for the purpose supplied at the church.

The Pastor and Trustees earnestly request that EVERY MEMBER of the church and congregation become a subscriber, and, as far as possible, adopt the envelope system of weekly payments.

The reverse side of the card might contain the following :

1. Every believer is bound by the positive command of God to give for His cause.

2. Each is required to give according to his ability.

3. Each is to give habitually, as he can thus do it most effectively, and that he may constantly honor God.

4. God calls for our gifts as a mark and as the measure of our love : " God loves a cheerful giver."

5. God makes the salvation of our fellow men dependent on our fidelity.

The other form of circular letter might be something like the following :

To the Members and Friends of the Main Street Lutheran Church :

DEAR BROTHER :

The Council of the church with which you have the privilege of being associated, after a careful survey of the whole field, find that it will require the sum of $... to pay our pastor's salary, and to meet all the other expenses of the church for the current year. This sum, if divided equally among our entire membership, would be $ per annum, or   cents per week for each member. This amount, though above the ability of some, is doubtless much less than others can pay, so that the average may safely be relied upon, provided each will give in accordance with the Scripture rule—"as God hath prospered him"—not less than one-tenth, and as much more as the prosperity of the week will enable him.

To secure this average weekly contribution, and to do it, too, in such a way as will be most easy for yourselves, your brethren of the Church Council have determined to introduce and to thoroughly test what is known in church financiering as "The Envelope System."

Hoping that you will cordially co-operate with us in this effort, and that as soon as convenient you will notify us by letter or otherwise, of the amount you will probably contribute weekly, we have enclosed to you, in connection with this circular, a package of fifty-two envelopes, each of which contains your register number, with a blank for date and amount of contribution.

Into one of these envelopes we ask you to deposit weekly the amount you feel you ought to give for the support of the church, and having dated it, and placed on it the amount enclosed, deposit the whole in the basket on Sabbath morning or evening. Or if you cannot be present at the service, send your envelope by the hand of a friend, or else double the amount the following Sabbath. And let this be done, week by week, till you have formed the habit, like the worship-

19

ers of ancient times, of always taking with you an offering of some kind whenever you appear in the courts of the Lord's house. By doing this you will be personally benefited, the treasury of the church will be able to meet all the demands against it, special efforts will be avoided, and the cause of Christ saved from reproach and greatly advanced.

Confidently relying upon your co-operation in the plan adopted, we subscribe ourselves,

Your brethren in Christ.

January 1, 188 . THE CHURCH COUNCIL.

A SYSTEM UNITING THE LOCAL AND FOREIGN WORK.

As some pastors prefer a system which will provide for both the home and foreign work, we present in full a system introduced by Rev. W. T. Wylie, and known as

THE BELLEFONTE METHOD.

There are two sets of cards, or, for greater convenience, one card printed on both sides. On one side, under the head of "Support of the Gospel," an estimate is made of the money required for the year, including pastor's salary, sexton's services, Sabbath-school work, fuel, light, repairs, etc. This divided by 365 gives how much is needed every day for the year. This result divided by the number of communicants shows the average per day required of each. Some, of course, can give far more than this average amount, while others fall below it. The contributions of friends, adherents and children, in addition to communicants, will almost certainly secure the average required.

The second side is for the " Spread of the Gospel." No estimate of any amount is placed on this, but each communicant is enjoined to give, as God enables, a daily sum, to which from time to time may be added as a special contribution whatever the giver is able to set apart. Every friend is also invited to join in this. The sum total of this fund is before the session, who appropriate as they think best to the different boards and other claims which are brought before the church, and report their action to the congregation.

Two sets of envelopes accompany these cards One package of twelve, or one for each month, of a dark color, is furnished by the trustees. The other package also contains twelve envelopes of a light color, the different colors being used to distinguish them.

The cards are distributed to the congregation, and given to every member and adherent, and also the children of church members. The object is explained, and each is urged to make his duty a matter of careful and prayerful study, and then to fill up the blanks in each card, sign his name, and return on the next Sabbath. It is very important that families so divide their contributions that each member, even the little child, has some share in the work.

When the cards are returned, the names are entered in the treasurer's book, together with the sum subscribed by each. Then twenty-four envelopes are placed with each card in a neat box prepared for this purpose (twelve dark for Church Support, and twelve light for Spread of the Gospel), and given to the person whose name is on the card. On the back of each envelope is written the person's name, as on the card. At the close of each month every individual places the amount of his contribution in the envelope, seals it, and drops it into the collection on Sabbath. The treasurer opens the envelopes, credits each with the payment made, and thus the work goes on to the close of the year.

In case some members of the church have not sent in their cards at the first, as is likely to occur through delay or carelessness, they should be called on by a committee of session for the work of benevolence and by a committee of trustees for church support.

Not one member of the church should be left whose name is not enrolled as giving, if only one cent a day.

Advantages of the System.—These are numerous and decided, both as to the individual giving and the cause. They are even more important in a spiritual point of view than in a pecuniary.

1. Every one is called to do his share in the Lord's work.

2. Each gives in the easiest way—day by day, little by little.

3. Each is called to exercise conscience, and act habitually as towards God, thus educating himself in God's work.

4. Daily thought and daily prayer are directed to our first great work in life, sustaining and spreading the Lord's cause.

5. The session can see just how each member is performing his duty.

6. There is no annoyance from collectors, each being his own collector, and the account can be prepared so that a glance will show how it stands.

7. The poorest member of the church can do his share just as well as the wealthiest, and feel that all are helpers of Christ's work, " e·ch as God enables."

How to Introduce the System.—Let the session and trustees each examine the method pertaining to their several departments.

It is better to adopt and introduce them at once, but if the trustees prefer some other way, the session may adopt and work the scheme for the benevolent contributions of the church.

When the plan is decided on, get your cards printed so as to have one for each man, woman and child in the bounds of the congregation.

Distribute on a Sabbath when there is a full attendance, and collect on the next Sabbath ; be prompt in getting all the cards in, then fill out your treasurer's roll, prepare and distribute the envelopes, and keep the business up square.

We append also a brief extract from another very excellent development of the same plan, prepared by " Z. W. B." and published in the *Congregationalist:*

" In our local field we have to provide (1) for the public preaching of the gospel in G d's house, for the prayer-meetings, for the Sabbath-school, and for the various other agencies which a *live* church will employ in strengthening itself and in reaching the community around ; and (2) for aiding the poor wh m God's providence has placed among us. The ormer, including warming, lighting and care of the house, pastor's salary, etc., will cost say $5,000. As the Master's command is to preach the gospel to the perishing, and as the whole tenor and spirit of the New Testament shows that He would have the poorest and humblest sinner made welcome to come and listen to the glad tidings of salvation (' to the poor the gospel is preached '), so we should have no *caste* in the house of the Lord (see James ii. 2, 3), no *exclusive* pews, no hired or purchased seats, but every seat should be free, whosoever will, may come and take of the water of life freely. This will necessitate regular contributions. If all the three hundred persons whose names are on the church records could be counted as 'paying' members, thirty-two cents a week from each would meet this demand ; but as, for various reasons, a large number cannot be so counted, let us suppose that two hundred and fifty will be regular contributors ; then it will take an average of thirty-nine cents a week from each.

" For the relief work and local charities a competent relief committee could expend to advantage $500 during the year. Four cents a week from each paying member will give this."

The Home Missionary Work, the Foreign Missionary Work, the Work Among the Seamen, and the Distribution of Bibles and Religious Literature—each is presented clearly and fully in a lengthy but most excellent circular, and the claims of each cause is estimated as follows :

I. *The Local Work.*
    For church expenses, per week......39c.
    For Relief Fund..... .... 4c.
                     —— 43c.

II. *The Home Missionary Work.*
    For Home Missionary Society....... $2\frac{1}{2}$c.
    For American Missionary Association $2\frac{1}{2}$c.
    For Congregational Union.......... 1c.
    For College and Education Society... 1c.
                     —— 7c.

III. *The Foreign Work.*
    For A. B. C. F. M................ $3\frac{1}{2}$c.

IV. *The Work Among the Seamen.*
    For Seaman's Friend Society . . . .   1c.
V. *The Distribution of Bibles and Relig-*
      ious Literature.
    For Bible Society . . . . 1c.
    For Congregational Pub. Society . . . . 1c.
    For Tract Society . . . . 1c.
                                      —— 3c.

                                          $57\frac{1}{2}$c.

" This would make the weekly sum for a family having two church members (the average number), $1.15,
amounting for the year to $59.80, which is the ' tithe '
of an income of $598, or five per cent. of an income of
$1,196. There are those among us who will undoubt-
edly (at least for the missionary objects) give twice,
thrice, five or ten times the amount named.

" The sum named for the local work (43 cents per
week, or $22.36 a year for each paying member) will
of course vary from these figures in those churches
where the membership bears a different ratio to
expenses. Thus a church having five hundred paying
members and the same expenses, would need but half
the sum named from each.

" For all the other channels of our work the sum
named (14$\frac{1}{2}$ cents a week, or $7.54 a year, for the
work in all the world) is the very lowest which will
pay our debts. And the size of the local church
makes no difference as to this. It is the minimum
which the ' paying members ' of any church should
average.

" *Pledges and Collections.*—For the efficient accomplishment of the object in view, we would propose that the church resolve itself into a missionary society. Let the executive committee procure a supply of cards something like that below, and distribute them to the members and among the congregation, together with a circular stating the needs of the church for the ensuing year.

WHAT I WILL DO FOR JESUS.

I will (God prospering me) give weekly at least the sum set against my name for the objects mentioned below (reserving, however, the right to cancel or change this pledge at any time, by due notice to the Treasurer, should it seem necessary for me to do so) :

CENTS.

For church expenses ....
For our church Relief Fund.............
For Home Missionary Society...........
For American Missionary Association.....
For Congregational Union...............
For College and Education Society........
For A. B. C. F. M......................
For Seamen's Friend Society............
For Bible Society..... ....
For Congregational Publication Society...
For Tract Society......................

Name .

Residence

After prayerfully and thoughtfully reading the accompanying circular, please fill out and sign above pledge, and place it in the contribution box next Sabbath.   20

" On the back of the card should be printed a statement of the average amount which should be given.

" Let numbered envelopes be issued to each one who shall sign a pledge (every child in the congregation should be encouraged to pledge its mite), and let the amount pledged for all the objects be placed in the envelopes weekly, and the envelopes be collected in the contribution box on the Sabbath. If any one wishes to add a free-will offering, either for the general work or for a special object, let him do so, stating the amount and object on the envelope."

FORMS FOR ENVELOPES.

Want of space prevents us from presenting but a few forms for envelopes. The following, however, may suffice by way of suggestion :

No. ....   *January.*

Trinity Lutheran Church,
MARTIN'S CREEK, PA.

TITHE-OFFERING,
FOR THE SUPPORT OF THE GOSPEL.

" Trust not in uncertain riches, but in the living God.—*1 Tim. vi. 17.*

" Remember the Lord thy God, for it is He that giveth thee power to get wealth."—*Deut. viii. 18.*

☞*Enclose the amount* REGULARLY, *seal, and place in the collection basket.*

WEEKLY CONTRIBUTION ENVELOPE

FOR THE

PRESBYTERIAN CHURCH,

DE PERE, WISCONSIN,

FOR PASTOR'S SALARY.

The church asks you to GIVE SOMETHING every Sabbath, "as God hath prospered you" (1 Cor. xvi. 2), to sustain His cause. Inclose it in this envelope, write your name on it, and drop it in the box in the vestibule or the collection box. When you cannot attend, send it.

"GOD LOVETH A CHEERFUL GIVER."

.*Name* _____

" Freely ye have received, freely give."—Matt. x. 8.

"Honor the Lord with thy substance."—Prov. iii. 9.

. "Upon the first day of the week let every one of you lay by him in store, as God hath prospered him."—*1 Cor. xvi. 2.*

FROM CONTRIBUTOR

No. 22.

SABBATH,

JANUARY 7th, 1880.

WEEKLY SUBSCRIPTION

TO THE

FOURTEENTH STREET PRESBYTERIAN CHURCH,

NEW YORK.

" Every man according as he purposeth in his heart, so let him give; not grudgingly, or of necessity; for God loveth a cheerful giver."—*2 Cor. ix. 7.*

MONTHLY OFFERING
FOR PASTOR.

Amount $

FIRST ENGLISH LUTHERAN CHURCH
PHOENIXVILLE, PA.

Month   188

From

THE TREASURER'S BOOK.

Procure a book properly ruled, with space on the left-hand margin for register number, a second space for the entry of names in alphabetical order, a third space for amount of subscription pledged, and fifty-two additional spaces for the entry of weekly contributions, or twelve for monthly contributions.*

If desirable, the classes can be arranged separately, leaving a hundred lines for each class—the members of the first class being registered from 100 to 199, the second from 200 to 299, &c., so that the first figure of the register number will always indicate the class to

*A very excellent, yet economical book, prepared especially for this purpose, may be had of I. K. Funk & Co.

which it belongs. The register number attached to a name on the treasurer's book is to be placed on the left-hand margin of the class-book, and also upon each of the envelopes given him for use. Any outside friends that contribute can be placed in a class by themselves, and registered accordingly.

In entering the several amounts contributed, the treasurer will work entirely by the numbers, and thus will find the task comparatively easy.

Statements should be sent out to each contributor annually, or oftener, showing the amount received; and a full statement of the finances of the church made to the whole congregation at the end of the year.

BILLS AND REMINDERS.

The amounts pledged should not be allowed to fall in arrears. If those whose pledges are not fully redeemed are called upon at least semi-annually, then any discrepancies in accounts can easily be adjusted before so long a time has elapsed that payments cannot be recalled.

Bills and reminders may be profitably used, but care should be taken lest they be used too liberally, or in such a manner as to lose their influence in accomplishing the desired result. We append a couple of forms :

Church of the Ascension.

REMINDER.

M

Your subscription appears to be   .....weeks
in arrears.

188   .

_____

M

To NINTH STREET BAPTIST CHURCH, Dr.

To Balance due on Subscription for Support of Worship, beginning April 1, 188   .

Dr. Amount of Subscription for   weeks $

Cr. By amount paid as per Treasurer's book

Balance due   -   -   -   -

Cincinnati,_____   188   .

Please give this your early attention.

_____

THE SCRIPTURAL METHOD.

God would not, and most assuredly did not, establish his church upon earth making no provision for
its perpetuation and support. In the very beginning
God instituted the giving of tithes for that purpose,
and the law of the tithe is as old as the church, as old
as the institution of the Sabbath, and as old as the

institution of sacrifices. It is not only as old as these, but is as universal and far-reaching as the human race, and its binding force sweeps on through each and all the centuries to the end of time.

Our position, then, is that the expenditures of the church are to be met by the payment upon the part of all people of *at least* one-tenth of all their income.

So many are the doubts, misapprehensions and difficulties which have grown out of the heresies which have been both preached and printed on this subject since the thirteenth century, that its full and clear presentation will require more space than could be given to it in this place, and we therefore call the attention of the reader to the full consideration of this subject in the chapter on the " Tithe, Free-Will Offering and Alms-giving "

CONCLUSION.

Rev. George Harris, in presenting a system of weekly contributions now in quite general use in the State of Rhode Island, urges the necessity of a system and meets some of the objections in the following manner:

" The preacher may unfold with the utmost skill the principle that obligation is measured by ability; he may urge his hearers to set apart a fixed proportion of their income for the Lord, and if one man in the congregation adopts his eloquent advice, he thinks he has not preached in vain ; but let the sermon be accompanied by a concise little card which contains figures and directions, so that a child can understand, and there will be hundreds in every congregation who will respond. Precisely this course must be adopted, if giving throughout our congregations is to be measured by ability. Every church must put an actual, definite system, explained in a few printed words, into the hands of every man, woman and child, before any considerable number will give according to their ability. Good intentions cannot be trusted ; there must be an existing and visible system, and the principle, whatever the details, must be the pledge of some amount to be given during the year.

" When new plans of any kind are proposed to a church, opposition, or at least reluctance, is sure to be encountered. The people are naturally and justifiably shy of experiments. Yet, some experiments must be made, and this experiment of systematic giving must be made. If the pastor is timid, the system will not be introduced, or if introduced, will have only a moderate success ; but if the pastor exercises good-natured determination, he will soon gain the support of the church, and then if he presents the subject faithfully he will be astonished to find that so many in the congregation are ready to respond, and will blame himself for neglecting his duty so long.

" The earnest support of the pastor is necessary after a vote of the church has been given in favor of the new system. He will need in his preaching not only to state strong reasons for adopting the plan ; he will also need to meet objections which different individuals will bring forward to excuse themselves from making a pledge. More than one will say or think : · It is difficult to decide how much to give. I do not know what my income will be next year, nor, indeed, if I shall have any ; it is almost impossible in a large business to separate twelve months and compute the gains, because so many transactions cover a more extended period. Unforeseen expenditures may be necessary. I do not know what percentage I ought to give, at any rate. The pastor, either in his sermon or in private, must be ready to reply. He will say : ' If you are convinced of the correctness of the principle, it must be that there is some amount which you are morally certain you can give. For example, you are doubtful whether or not you can give one dollar a week; but you are certain you can give half a dollar—then give that, and make additions if you are able. Or, if you can decide in no other way, give as much as you have been in the habit of giving; get the whole amount and divide it by fifty-two for your weekly pledges. If you say, I do not know how much I have been giving, the remark

21

proves the need of a system ; you ought to know. Almost any one can make an estimate of usual income and necessary expenses, which, if not exact, will be nearly accurate. At any rate, whatever you give, you probably will not err in the direction of excess. The phenomenon has seldom been observed of a person who became embarrassed by giving too much.' A very good rule to recommend to such persons, and indeed to all, is that they make such a pledge as they honestly think is sufficient, and arrange their other expenses accordingly. First make some proper pledge, and then bring other outlays into conformity with it.

" Some will object that it is too much trouble to make these estimates and pledges, and to bring the money every Sunday ; but it will vanish, perhaps, when the pastor says : ' That objection I consider to be a recommendation ; we have not taken nearly trouble enough; the Lord expects us to take just this trouble, and to find it a pleasure. My on y fear is that you will not take the trouble you ought to take, that in some careless fashion you will put down fifty cents or a dollar without any thought at all. If ladies will take as much trouble as they take to match the trimmings for one dress, to which they patiently devote two or three mornings, the question of how much would be settled, and rightly settled ; if gentlemen will devote as much time to it as they devote to selecting cigars or to choosing a new coat, proper decisions would be reached.'

" Some will object, saying, what I can give is so little that it is not worth while to take the pledge and keep the account. But the cheery pastor reminds them that one of the chief recommendations of the system is that it swells small gifts into a large volume, and adds: 'Can you discover that your obligation to give a little, if it is all you can afford, is any less real than the obligation of one who can give largely? In the parable of the talents, which servant was condemned? It was he who had but one talent; so little that he went and hid it in the earth! Among those who cast their gifts into the treasury while Christ looked on, who was commended? It was the poor widow who cast in two mites, which make a farthing.'

" The pressure of hard times will be urged as an objection, to which the undismayed pastor will reply : 'Don't limit your retrenchments to your benevolence. It is not very consistent for a Christian to stop giving, and keep up all other outlays to the old standard.'

" For those who have had losses and are in debt, if they can give anything, it should be with a system, for such persons, above all others, should systematize their expenditures and benevolence.

" Any plan that may be proposed will be met with
some objections. This plan has fewer objections and
more recommendations than any plan of which we
know ; but so good a system as this, especially at its
introduction, must have the unhesitating support
of the pastor, or it will meet with little favor. But
can any pastor be satisfied with the shiftless, casual
habits of giving which so commonly prevail? Is it
not worth all the trouble he may take to develop the
latent resources of the congregation? Any pastor
who despises the details of practical Christian work
in his church, and devotes himself, as he says, to the
pulpit, has sadly curtailed his opportunities as a
Christian minister. The people wait for their pastor
to take the lead in every good work ; they often wonder why he does not devise plans of Christian benevolence, and appeal to them in behalf of suffering mis-
sionaries and of perishing men and women who need
the gospel. It is a shame for ministers to let their
churches go on in the old ruts, giving but a fragment
of what they might give, while our missionary societies are struggling with debt, and are obliged to with-
draw their workers from important fields. And so I
say that the essential condition for introducing a plan
of systematic beneficence is the unequivocal influence
of the pastors in its favor. Another important condition is the co-operation of those who have been the

large givers in a church. If they hold aloof, success will not be so certain ; but if they adopt the system for themselves and encourage their children to adopt it, there can be little doubt of signal success.

" If the pastor is an earnest advocate of it, and if those who already give adopt it, the system can easily be introduced to supplant the careless and unequal giving which is now so common."

CHAPTER V.

HOW TO KEEP CHURCHES OUT OF DEBT.

(*NEW ENTERPRISES.*)

DANGER IN NEW ENTERPRISES—PRACTICAL SUGGESTIONS—
HOW TO PROCEED—WHERE TO BUILD—PLANS—SPECIFI-
CATIONS AND CONTRACTS—HOW MUCH MONEY TO IN-
VEST—THE FINAL COST—THE SCRIPTURAL METHOD—
THE TABERNACLE AND TEMPLE, COST OF—REPAIRING
OF—SINKING-FUND PLAN—PASTORAL-LETTER PLAN—
JOINT-OWNERSHIP PLAN—JOINT-STOCK PLAN—A CATH-
OLIC PRIEST'S PLAN—A GOOD SUGGESTION—VARIOUS
OTHER PLANS.

It has truthfully been said that "change is dangerous," and to those experienced in the erection of new
church edifices it is unnecessary to say that it is a
developing period in the career of the congregation
which is fraught with difficulties and dangers, and
often with disasters, either to pastor or people, and often
to both. It is a time when those giving direction to
affairs, are called upon to exercise the utmost wisdom.
But the arduous labors and perplexing difficulties
should not be sources of discouragement, they should
rather awaken to greater effort and increased caution
in the work so necessary to be accomplished.

PRACTICAL SUGGESTIONS.

Here in the very beginning let us give a word of counsel to those who are to be leaders in carrying forward new enterprises. Unpleasantnesses are likely to arise, unkind things will be said, and unthought and unwrought plans and suggestions will be inflicted upon you, but never, under any circumstances whatever, allow yourself to lose that self-control which will restrain you from saying those things which will do no good, but result in positive evil. Never lose your temper. If insulted appear to be too stupid to be aware of it. Remember that men often regret what they did say, but seldom what they did not say. An insignificant seed when left to germinate will sever a rock, so a single expression, a word, or even a look, may and often has dismembered entire congregations.

While we would urge upon all such as desire to know how to keep churches out of debt the importance of a careful reading of each of the chapters herein presented, yet if this cannot be done we would call special attention to Chapter II., page 21, on " How Churches Get in Debt." In Chapter III., A Wrong Policy, page 54 ; Stopping the Evil, page 58 ; Selecting a Committee, page 64 ; Suggestions to Committees, page 64 ; Making Collections, page 68.

HOW TO PROCEED.

When a new undertaking is contemplated, the whole

matter should be presented so as to secure the best judgment and most hearty co-operation of all persons interested. Although the official board, or the trustées, or a committee are to be entrusted with the greater responsibilities of carrying forward the project yet they are only the servants of the people, and are dependent upon them for sympathy and support.

Having determined the necessity of a new church, parsonage or any other structure, one of the first things to be inquired into is, how much money can be secured for the object. Much caution is necessary just at this point, for many will promise, or even pledge much more than they are able ever to pay. Enthusiasm is apt to usurp the place of reason, and liberal impulses are liable to outrun financial ability. Some men will subscribe a thousand dollars who never had so much money at any one time. In a new enterprise many will follow their zeal, ambition, and even their pride, rather than their judgment. On the other hand again, many will be controlled by a parsimonious, illiberal spirit rather than by a sense of Christian duty. In endeavoring to reach such, the committee will need to select the best plan, and to go fortified with such arguments as will secure the desired amount, and at the same time leave the contributor a better and more liberal man.

22

WHERE TO BUILD.

When once it has been determined that a new church is to be erected, one of the first things to be considered is a proper site. A good location ought by all means to be secured. In a city the selection is often limited to a choice between two or three scanty lots; but it must be kept in mind in building city churches, as Bishop Asbury said, "If you are going to catch fish you must either go where they are, or where they are likely to come." But there are some considerations never to be lost sight of. Let the surroundings be such as will awaken only feelings of veneration. Often churches are built where the attitude of every building, and the uses to which they are employed are such as awaken anything but reverence, because they are discordant to every thought of Christian worship. Where circumstances will allow, other things being equal, a corner lot is much to be preferred, as it will allow the church to front on two streets, giving easy entrance and exit, besides affording better light and ventilation. Among the many other things to be looked after, due regard should be paid to a location where the service will not be interrupted by the rumbling of wheels over the hard pavement of the street, or the noise of passing street cars, or railroad trains. Avoid a proximity to buildings of such magnitude as will mar the architectural proportions of the church

by their overshadowing uncomeliness, or will cut off a
good supply of light and ventilation. Where space
sufficient can be secured it is by far preferable to
place the building back from the street, so as to afford
space for an ample court. In large cities, where the
cost of land is excessive, it is not always possible to
stand the church back from the street, but the effect
is often marred by this necessity.

It is often the case that a church site is tendered to
a congregation free of charge. This may be a for-
tunate or an unfortunate event, according to circumstances. It is sometimes found to be the case that
some wealthy parishioner desires to improve the value
of adjacent property by the near proximity of a fine
church, erected at the expense of others. In this way
some men try to appear generous, while they are
purely selfish. In the country, where land is comparatively cheap, the church should occupy the best
site the vicinity affords. Let the space be ample, and
by all means avoid barren, bleak, treeless locations,
exposed to the driving storms and winds in winter,
and the pitiless heat in summer. Let the location be
central and desirable, not selected because remoteness
and barrenness render it cheap.

When once the site has been determined upon,
let the architect look over the ground and surroundings so that he may submit such a draft as shall be

best adapted to that particular location, for a structure that would be adapted to one location might be
entirely unsuited to another.

THE PLAN, OR DRAFT.

Unless you have an abundance of money at command, and desire to erect something different from
the seventy-five thousand church edifices in the United
States, we would recommend that you beware of experiments. Select a church which is suited to your wants
and then use it as a model. Among the thousands
already constructed, of such various styles of architecture, ranging in cost from $150 to $300,000, some
one or more will be suited to your wants. "Their
sizes, proportions, materials and cost may be easily
obtained, and will indicate which is to be preferred, all
things considered. It is not difficult to find churches
constructed for $10,000 that will be justly preferred
to others which cost twice that amount. Some of
them are perfect charms, beautiful, easy to speak and
hear in, and in every way attractive and inviting, while
others are as notably defective. It is folly to expect
any architect to excel the best of them, particularly
in their accoustic properties. Churches differ radically
in this particular, and no architect can tell why. In
some the lowest voice can be heard in every part;
while in others of the same size the loudest is indis-
tinct, and hearing difficult, if not impossible. The

only sure way to success in this respect is to select a model that has been fully tested, and follow it. The importance of this point cannot be overestimated. It has more to do with the health, happiness and usefulness of the preacher, and the size of the congregation than is generally imagined. For him to strain his voice to make himself heard, and fail, is killing, not only to him, but the people; they will soon leave him."*

In selecting a model avoid all such as are cold, unsocial and unsuited to the true spirit of devotion. A church should present an attractive, genial, home-like appearance, and yet not lack that which reminds us that we are in a sacred place.

SPECIFICATIONS AND CONTRACT.

When the proper model has been selected, in *most instances* it will be found advisable to secure an architect to give an accurate draft of every part of the building, giving, also, such specifications as will include every stick of timber, amount of lumber, number of bricks, style of finish, form of pulpit and pews, and everything down to the minutest details. This expense and delay will save both time and money. It will give the builders an intelligible basis for an economical estimate, and then if the contract is explicit in all of its details, as it

*Rev. James Porter, D. D.

always should be, it will protect the congregation against all bills for extras. Contract only with reliable parties, and such as are able to complete the work without loading the structure with builders' liens; and then, if the contract is clear and explicit in every detail, the church may be completed without perplexing annoyances, litigations and final disgust.

HOW MUCH MONEY TO INVEST.

Invest all the money you can raise, but not more. Build as beautiful and costly a church as you can pay for,* but in making your plans, if you would be on the safe side, make a full allowance for unredeemable pledges, and double the amount which is estimated to be sufficient to complete the building. Do not build for posterity, for in nine cases out of ten posterity will tear down your structure to build one more agreeable to its own taste. Build for yourselves, and leave "posterity" to do the same. Build a church to meet your needs, and not one that shall be "an ornament to the city." Amomg churches we have already too many ornaments, and too few which are well suited to the purposes for which churches should be built.

THE FINAL COST.

The cases are rare where the final expense does not exceed, to a surprising extent, the figures primitively stated as the ultimatum. The diversity, of course,

*See also Chapter II., section 4, page 27.

varies with the foresight exercised by those in charge
of the enterprise. But it may be stated as a rule, to
which there are few exceptions, that the first estimates
fall far short of the final cost. Although these facts
may tend to discourage, they will, when properly
taken into account, occasion less embarrassment, and
be more easily surmounted, "for he who is forewarned
is forearmed." Where a chapel is to cost $1,000 it is
often the case that unthought of expenditures increase
this amount to twice that sum. Where the church is
estimated at $40,000, an additional $20,000 or $30,000
is usually required to pay for alterations in plan, improvements, or to meet expenditures required, but
overlooked from the first. If these facts affright the
committee or congregation, be consoled with the
thought that it is better to be appalled before, rather
than after the debt is created. Be consoled also with
the thought that most congregations can, with proper
management, do from two to six times more than the
various members anticipated they could possibly afford.

THE SCRIPTURAL PLAN.

The first account we have in the Scriptures of any
building erected for the worship of God, is the *tabernacle*. The account (Ex. xxxv.–xl.) is briefly this :
When on the mount, Moses received from the Lord
the command to build the tabernacle, which the children of Israel were to carry with them as they re-

moved from place to place in their journeys through the wilderness.

" And Moses spake unto all the congregation of the children of Israel, saying, This is the thing which the Lord commanded, saying, Take ye from among you an offering unto the Lord : whosoever is of a willing heart, let him bring it, an offering of the Lord ; gold, and silver, and brass, and blue, and purple, and scarlet, and fine linen, and goats' hair, and rams' skins dyed red, and badgers' skins, and shittim wood, and oil for the light, and spices for annointing oil, and for the sweet incense, and onyx stones, and stones to be set for the ephod, and for the breastplate, and every wise-hearted among you shall come, and make all that the Lord hath commanded."

" And they came, every one whose heart stirred him up, and every one whom his spirit made willing, and they brought the Lord's offering to the work of the tabernacle of the congregation, and for all his service, and for the holy garments. And they came, both men and women, as many as were willing hearted, and brought bracelets, and earrings, and rings, and tablets, all jewels of gold : and every man that offered, offered an offering of gold unto the Lord."

And the workmen " received of Moses all the offering, which the children of Israel had brought for the work of the service of the sanctuary, to make it withal. And they brought yet unto him free offerings every morning. And all the wise men, that wrought all the work of the sanctuary, came every man from his work which they made ; and they spake unto Moses, saying, The people being much more than enough for the service of the work which the Lord commanded to make. And Moses gave commandment, and they caused it to be proclaimed throughout the camp, saying, Let neither man nor woman make any more work for the offering of the sanctuary. So the people were restrained from bringing. For the stuff they had was sufficient for all the work to make it, and too much."

" All the gold that was occupied for the work in all the work of the holy place, even the gold of the offering, was twenty and nine talents, and seven hundred and thirty shekels, after the shekel of the sanctuary. And the silver of them that were numbered of the congregation was a hundred talents, and a thousand seven hundred and threescore and fifteen shekels, after the shekel of the sanctuary. A bekah for every man, that is, half a shekel, after the shekel of the sanctuary, for every one that went to be numbered, from twenty years old and upward, for six hundred thousand and three thousand five hundred and fifty men. * * *

" And the brass of the offering was seventy talents, and two thousand and four hundred shekels."

Dr Adam Clarke tells us that this would be 4,245 pounds of gold, 14,602 pounds of silver, and 10,277 pounds of brass, troy weight. This, reduced to avoirdupois weight, makes nearly ten and a half tons. The gold would amount to $960,002.50 ; the silver, $219,-088.64 ; the brass (at one English shilling per pound), $2,487.03, making a total of $1,171,578.17.

If we add to these figures the value of the many other offerings brought by every one " whose heart stirred him up, and every one whom his spirit made willing," we may get some idea of the cost of the first building erected for the public worship of God, of which we have any record. We should also remember that the scarcity of the precious metals at that early period rendered them so much the more to be prized by their possessors. The gold which had been employed in the golden calf had all been destroyed, and yet so freely and cheerfully did the people respond that they had to be told, as morning after morning they came with their offerings, that there was already more than enough—they even had to be " *restrained from bring-ing.*"

There are at least three reasons why such vast wealth should have been used in the construction of the tabernacle : (*a.*) To impress the minds of the peo-ple with the glory of the Divine Majesty, and the esti-mate which was to be placed upon His service. (*b.*) To convert the spoils which they had brought out of Egypt into the blessed means of rendering them lib-eral and cheerful givers, while at the same time they unburdened their hands of that which was liable to become the occasion of covetousness. (*c.*) To prevent pride and vain-glory, by giving for the divine service those ornaments of person which would have had a direct tendency to divert their minds from sacred things.

Later in the sacred history we find that when the temple of Solomon was built, the free-will offerings of the people were poured in such astonishing profusion that we fail to comprehend the value of such vast treasures. When David instructed Solomon (I. Chron. xxii: 14,) concerning the building of the temple, already he had " prepared for the house of the Lord a hundred thousand talents of gold ($2,456,678,125,) and a thousand thousand talents of silver " ($1,711,-383,666.) To this various additions were made, until the vast masses of gold and silver become almost incalculable. The various authorities differ greatly. Among the lowest is our own calculation of $4,396,-606,465. One, of credible authority, whose estimate is not among the highest, states the amount at $35,-520,000,000, making 48,000 tons of gold and silver. Now, if this latter amount be correct, and all this precious metal were to be loaded on wagons bearing one ton each, allowing twenty feet space for each wagon to move in the procession, the unbroken line would reach from New York to Harrisburg, a distance of 182 miles.

If this seems startling, turn to I. Kings, vi. and vii., and read the description of this costly structure with " the whole house overlaid with gold," and " the floor of the house overlaid with gold, within and without." All *ordinary* things may be overstated, but there are some things so vast that words are crushed beneath the freightage which they must bear to convey even the idea from mind to mind. Niagara never has been, and can never be described. Words cannot make the mountains of Switzerland arise in their towering magnitude before the mind, or convey any idea of the vast proportions of St. Peter's, at Rome. The Queen of Sheba had heard very wonderful things concerning the beauty of Jerusalem, the glory of the temple and the wisdom of Solomon. The reports seemed so exaggerated that she affirmed that she could not believe them until she should see them with her own eyes, and yet, when she came, she declared that even the half had not been told her.

What unbounded prosperity and blessing did the people of God enjoy when they obeyed the injunction: " Honor the Lord with thy substance, and with the first fruits of all thine increase; So shall thy barns be filled with plenty, and thy presses shall burst out with new wine."

" There was never a moment when obedience did not bring affluent prosperity, and when disobedience did not bring destructive curse. Never before or afterward were such immense exactions called for as during the period in which the temple was built. And yet there was prosperity, material and spiritual, during that period such as had never been before and never was again. The people came up to the full measure of the legal requirements, and God poured in upon them material wealth like a mighty river. And afterwards, when decline came upon the nation, in every attempt made to revive it, the people were reminded, and everything was made of the fact, that for a long time the *offerings* had been neglected. And the decline was attributed to the divine displeasure upon the nation for this neglect. This reminder marks the revival under Hezekiah and that under Nehemiah, and, in fact, every revival and attempt at revival."*

Repairing the Temple.—During the reign of Jehoash, when the temple was in need of repairs, Jehoiada had a chest placed by the altar of sacrifice, and as the people prayed they proved their sincerity by their offerings for the repair of the Lord's house. When Joash, King of Juda, repaired the temple, a chest was made and set " without at the gate of the house of the Lord," into which the people might cast their offerings ; and " the king's scribe and the high priest's officer came and emptied the chest, and took it, and carried it to his place again. Thus they did day by day, and gathered money in abundance."

So also during the reign of the good King Josiah the offerings of the people were gathered by the " keepers of the door." So it was again, when poor and few in number, the Jews returned from Babylon, they gave liberally and worked faithfully for the rebuilding of the temple. Never was there a debt but provision was made before the work was begun, and when the topmost stone was brought on, it was with shouting, Grace, grace unto it !

*Rev. David Cole, D. D., in " Offerings to the Lord."

SINKING FUND PLAN.

When a congregation foresees the approaching necessity of repairing or rebuilding their church edifice, they would do well to follow the method pursued by Jehoiada, Joash, Josiah and all others who pursue a careful and judicious course. If the money cannot all be gathered at once, a fixed amount may be laid by at stated intervals until an amount is accumulated sufficient to meet the necessities of the case. In securing money for a new enterprise the people are not so apt to weary of the sinking fund plan as in raising a *debt*, even though it should extend through a series of years.

A working, energetic pastor in the city of New York who had secured the partial use of church edifices in which to gather the people for service, succeeded in collecting a membership of nearly six hundred communicants. The gifts of the poor toward the fund for the building of a church of their own aggregated about $1,500, when the pastor inaugurated the following plan. In writing of it the author, Rev. G. U. Wenner, says:

" The details of the plan we will explain. The amount required for a church is about $24,000. The working members of the church number about six hundred. Each member must, therefore, collect or contribute about $40. This, it is true, is a large sum for poor people these hard times. But we have given each member a contribution card containing twenty names and asked them to get ten cent contributions. The object is to get a small contribution from a large number of persons, in this case twelve thousand. The immediate effort is to enlist the hearty support of the entire parish. An immense number of persons by a small contribution, become pledged, as it were, to the final success of the enterprise. Such a collection can be made without any trouble two or three times a year, and in three or four years, who shall say that we will not have money enough to pay for our church? And then, what is better than the money, there will be a large number who feel that they have a claim on that church and can tell their children : ' There, that is our church. We helped to build that church.' "

Many of the methods presented in Chapter III. could be successfully used in securing a building fund. See also the sinking-fund plan considered in its relation to securing funds for paying church *debts*, page 80.

PASTORAL LETTER PLAN.

This plan has already been presented on page 87, and it remains only to present a specimen adapted to securing money for *new* enterprises, and to add a word as to its advantages.

The following letter was used several years ago by a very prominent pastor in the State of New York,

and in response to this letter several times the anticipated amount was pledged.   Good as the letter is, the
subscriptions which it secured were the result of the
preaching which had preceded it :

[CONFIDENTIAL.]

It is proposed to build a meeting-house and other
rooms for the use of the church.   To do this work
honestly and well, it is proposed to spend *one year* in
raising a part of the money *in advance;* and in getting plans and making contracts.

One year—plans and contracts...April 1, 1871, to '72
"   "   build and cover in....   "   1872, " '73
"   "   plaster, finish and fur-
             nish............. ....   "   1873, " '74
"   "   pay for in full and ded-
             icate..... ....   "   1874, " '75

It is proposed to expend not less than twenty thousand dollars nor more than fifty thousand—according
to the ability shown by the return of these cards of
confidential subscription.   Any member of the church
and congregation or any friend of the church is
allowed and invited to subscribe. But no one is urged.

——————————*Pastor.*

To help build our meeting-house I think that I shall
be able to give
Not less than $ and
Not more than $
Each year for four years, beginning April 1, 1871.
Or I can make in one payment $
Trusting in the Lord to help me, I hereby subscribe
the same as noted above.

Name ___

Residence

This plan is "free from certain faults which are conspicuous in nearly all existing methods. For example, it is entirely independent of personal solicitation, which from any point of view is an unmixed evil. Contributions for important objects in many of our churches are gathered by two or three self-sacrificing individuals, who go from house to house, and from office to office, to solicit donations. It is a laborious and vexatious undertaking. Those who go about on such an errand must falter out apologies for intrusion, must often receive ungracious replies or refusals, as though they had asked a personal favor, and even when received politely must make some sacrifice of self respect; and on the other hand, those who are solicited have ground of complaint. The collector may call at a time when they cannot give his claims due attention, they must decide while the collector stands before them with paper in hand, they must not give less than others have given, or less than they gave last year. Personal solicitation is an evil which can be truly characterized only by calling it a nuisance. It is almost fatal to a genuine benevolence to give only when asked; and it is a shame to send *any* persons on these begging expeditions, whether they are young ladies, who should be forbidden to go on such errands, or the pastors of our societies, who ought to be allowed to devote their time to better work. Such a

24

system is free from this grave objection. Each one decides *for* himself and *by* himself. He may take a week or two for reflection."

JOINT-OWNERSHIP PLAN.

The joint-ownership plan consists in an agreement upon the part of those interested to subscribe to the building fund, with the condition that the value of the subscription be returned, upon the completion of the building, in a title-deed to one or more pews. An opportunity is given also to new-comers, after the edifice is completed, to share in the property by purchase of pews. A Presbyterian pastor in New York city says of it : " This is a safe business arrangement provided—

"1. That the full amount needed is thus subscribed in advance.

"2. That the pew-owners will be responsible, each for his share of the expense of support, so long as they own pews.

"3. That the church is not hampered by the terms of the title-deeds in regard to the amount of annual tax to be assessed.

" But usually the full amount is not subscribed nor the pews all sold, and the result is : (*a.*) Two classes of pew-holders—owners and lessees. (*b.*) Two grades of assessments. We have known churches where the assessment upon pews held in fee was fixed forty years ago at an insignificant rate, and thus three-quarters of the expenses of the church came upon the minority of the congregation, who, as new-comers, *rented* pews. (c.) Pew-owners leaving the church abandon their property if unsalable. Morally, and we believe legally, they are still under obligations to the amount of the annual assessment, but the obligation is not likely to be enforced."

This plan was at one time quite generally used among the Presbyterian churches in the State of New York, but the principles upon which it rests and the difficulties it has encountered have caused it to be largely superseded by other methods.

The objections are: (a.) That the success of the enterprise is made to rest upon worldly and selfish principles, rather than upon the scriptural principle of giving our offerings and church to God. (b.) It is likely to occasion much difficulty when the old rights of proprietorship are encroached upon by any remodeling of the church, or the replacing of the old structure by a new one. (c.) Persons who have become offended, under the protection of their individual proprietorship, not desiring to attend worship have nailed their pews shut, or taken an axe and chopped their seats into kindling-wood.

For a consideration of this plan in relation to meeting the annual expenses of the church, see page 125.

JOINT-STOCK PLAN.

Had it not been for that which was meant for temporal wisdom, but which is everlasting folly, no such devices as the joint-ownership, joint-stock and other plans would ever have been known of. The necessity of resorting to such means is only a pitiable chapter upon the folly of the Church in departing from the scriptural principles and motives which are designed to influence men to do their duty in providing structures where they may together worship God.

The joint-stock plan is simply this : Capitalists unite to furnish the money to build the church, and in return for their money, accept scrip, or a certificate of stock, bearing the legal interest of the State. The certificates, or scrip, may be drawn so as to create a claim upon the edifice, or only upon the society as such, or upon the members of the society as individuals. The interest, to prevent any speculation in the stock, may be simply credited upon the pew rent each year, or it may be payable in cash, in which event the income of the church would have to be sufficient to pay the current expenses and the interest in addition.

The objections are : (a.) The congregation will not own its church home. (b., "The stockholders may include in their number irreligious men, whose only interest in the enterprise is a financial one. (c.) The church, in the management of its affairs, becomes in a measure subject to the stockholders. (*d.*) The church must be a financial success, which fact tends towards sensationalism and the valuation of a minister, whatever his character otherwise, by his ability to 'draw,' and thus make the stock pay dividends." (*e.*) It will lack those scriptural principles which will entitle it to the divine favor and blessing.

A CATHOLIC PRIEST'S PLAN.

Father Maguire, of the Roman Catholic Church, gathered a congregation in North Albany, N. Y. In two years the little temporary chapel was no longer able to contain the audiences, until one Sunday, after presenting the necessities of the parish, Father Maguire said to his people: "We will build a plain, cheap edifice, in which we may have room for every necessity. Material is cheap, labor is cheap, while many poor men will be glad to get employment; and by doing what we can ourselves we may make the burden light. To-morrow evening we shall break ground. Let each man of this congregation come to the church lots on Pearl street, bringing his shovel, pick, wheelbarrow, or horse and cart, and we shall work together each night until nine o'clock. Thus beginning in the name of God, we shall soon have made the excavations, and throughout as far as our strength or money permits we shall push on the work to completion."

At the appointed time about three hundred members
of the congregation assembled at the site of the new
church, armed with pick and shovel, ready for work.
The pastor, standing in their midst, uttered a blessing,
and then, as he thrust his shovel into the ground, the
scene became one of the greatest enthusiasm. Shout
after shout arose from the assembled crowd, and the
picks and shovels were plied most lively. Each evening from seven until nine o'clock this work was pushed
forward, and when Saturday night came, that part of
the work was complete, without any comparative cost.
In a somewhat similar manner the remainder of the
work was carried forward, until a church 124x64 stood
complete. It surely was a sensible and successful
method for a poor congregation to pursue.

A GOOD SUGGESTION.

In repairing and beautifying his church, Rev. J. H.
Leeser very aptly made such a division of the work
and expense as would most readily secure the co-operation of the different classes of people in the congregation. The young men and young women would be
most likely to labor faithfully for the adorning of the
church, so they were organized into a committee on
frescoing. The younger members of the congregation
were to secure the money for paying the plasterers.
The ladies secured the money for the new carpets, and
the older male members of the church paid the paint-

ers and built the new fence. Each of these classes
had its own treasurer and an executive committee, of
which the pastor was always chairman, and to secure
harmony of action, there was also a general committee, composed of one of each of the separate committees. The effect was stimulating to each department,
and the result most satisfactory. Among others,
there is one most excellent feature in this method, and
that is that it sets every one at work. If you want
your people interested in the church, give them something to do.

OTHER PLANS.

As much that relates to the subject of how to keep
new enterprises out of debt has already been presented
in Chapter III., on " How to Pay Church Debts," we
refer the reader to that department of our subject.

The advantages and disadvantages of the subscription plan, together with forms, &c., will be found on
page 61.

Note subscription plan, page 69.

Tax-list plan, page 74.

Apportioning plan, page 77.

Share plan, page 78.

Envelope subscription plan, page 79.

Helping plan, page 85.

Monthly collection plan, page 90.

Defrauding plan, page 93.

Church entertainment plan, page 95.

CHAPTER VI.

HOW TO RAISE MONEY FOR MISSIONS, AND BENEVOLENT WORK.

THE REQUIREMENTS—NEED OF SYSTEM—GIVING TO CHRIST, NOT TO SOCIETIES—WHERE MOST METHODS FAIL—RESULTS OF SYSTEM IN GIVING—ANNUAL COLLECTION PLAN—ANNUAL SUBSCRIPTION — QUARTERLY COLLECTION—A QUARTERLY SUBSCRIPTION PLAN—MONTHLY CONTRIBUTION PLANS—BY CIRCULAR LETTER—SUGGESTIVE FIGURES — CONTRIBUTION SCHEDULE — WEEKLY CONTRIBUTION PLANS—BASKET COLLECTION—AN ENVELOPE PLAN—WEEKLY OFFERINGS—FORMS, &c.—PLANS FOR DAILY OFFERINGS—THE FOUNDATION PLAN—THE BOX SYSTEM—CONTRIBUTION BOXES AT CHURCH DOORS — PRIVATE TREASURY FOR OFFERINGS — FORMS OF PLEDGES—CONCLUSION.

The ends to be attained by means of the beneficence of the church are the grandest in the accomplishment of which man is permitted to co-operate. In saving the world we become co-laborers with a God who declares himself as "a God of order." Harmony of action, therefore, demands that the human part of the work should be undertaken and carried forward orderly and systematically. Business men who aim to accomplish any considerable result prudently incorporate in their plans much of system. The church

25

should not be less prudent, for the vast work to be accomplished calls for organized and systematized effort.

In our own country many of the Western States and Territories are almost destitute of religious influences, to say nothing of the destitute districts in our large cities and open country. The isles of the sea and nations of the earth are to receive the Word of God at the hands of our beneficence, or remain in heathen darkness and spiritual death. The church of Christ is to accomplish a gigantic work, with most glorious results, and to this end there must of necessity be orderly arrangements and systematic workings.

Some are wont to ignore and others to decry system in bringing the church up to her privilege in this matter, and prefer to leave it to the impulse or inclination of those who give. They regard the results of successful church work as the child regards the motion of the hands across the face of the clock—having no idea of the hidden motive power and the relation of nicely adjusted spring, lever and wheel to moving hands. The unthinking and untaught see nothing to suggest order in the arrangement of the earth and heavens, but the student of God's handiwork stands with awe and reverence as investigation reveals the system of crystal, layer and strata, or as science draws aside the curtain of night to reveal group, cluster, nebula and ulterior systems, each moving with such nicety of adjustment that not the fraction of a second is lost in the onward course of the centuries.

The crippled financial condition of the religious boards and charitable societies is a natural result of the lack of system in securing the contributions of the individual members of the various denominations of Christian workers. Giving will not become systematic of itself. It must be made systematic; and this implies order and method. Too many congregations have absolutely no system at all. Others adopt such methods as gnaw at the very heart, and kill every principle of true benevolence. Any plan which parades names and amounts, and seeks to induce people to contribute *because* it will be blazed abroad, or prompts one to contribute an amount equal, or greater, than that given by another, that they may *appear* more generous in the eyes of the world, is false and ruinous in its effects. There is no objection to publicity, if publicity is not made the motive power in obtaining the contribution. When Christ said, " Let not thy left hand know what thy right hand doeth," he did not mean that our giving was to be kept a secret ; " He meant that the right hand should not steal around to the left, and, shaking it furtively, whisper behind your back : ' How generous I am ; how liberal I was just now.' But our Lord meant that the right hand should know what it is itself doing. He did not say, Let not thy right hand know what thy right hand doeth. He meant, Don't keep telling yourself how generous you are."

GIVING TO CHRIST, NOT TO SOCIETIES.

To the great mass of contributors the blessedness of giving is entirely lost. They are caused or permitted to feel that they contribute to maintain some struggling enterprise of Christian work. They do not give, as to the Lord, and therefore regard the act as one of merit. In the benevolent operations of the church we seem largely to overlook the fact that God does not of *necessity* call upon individual Christians for pecuniary, or any other sort of aid, in the prosecution of his work upon the earth. He might employ angels to herald his gospel, or trace his will upon the heavens in characters of unfading light. If he saw fit, he might speak the word, and the unearthed treasures of California would be at his service. He might demand, and the wealth of the world would have to be laid at his feet.

Some seek to evade their duty to contribute to the support of Foreign Mission work by arguing within themselves that the results, as compared with the money and lives invested, are not sufficient to prove the "experiment" of Christianizing the heathen a success. Christ says, "Go ye into all the world, and preach the gospel to every creature;" and as his followers we are simply to do as he commands. With the result we have nothing to do. God will take care of his part of the work. Christ does not ask for our *opinion*, but for our money. Not for Missions. but for himself. If we give to Missions, or Church Extension, or Bible, or Tract Society, we would look to them for our reward, which we will never receive. If we contribute as directly unto Christ, in an act of solemn worship, we may look to him for a reward which he will never fail to bestow. When we contribute as unto Christ we shall be ashamed to offer him a dime when we should come with dollars. We shall not withhold for fear the money will not be properly applied or judiciously expended. If we give to Christ we shall look to him, and not to committees, to direct and use it. If we deposit it in Christ's purse, and Judas steals it, the responsibility is not with us. We have given it to Christ and there our responsibility ends as far as the duty of giving is concerned.

WHERE MOST METHODS FAIL.

The failure of most methods is due to the fact that they fail to reach the masses. When large revenues are to be secured in any government, it is done by imposts and duties so levied as to reach *all* classes. The vast revenues necessary for the support of the various governments are drawn from the masses of the people, and perhaps the greater burden is usually borne by those in more moderate circumstances, and by the poorer classes. The experiment, attempted soon after the close of the war, of paying our national debt by the voluntary contributions of the rich, proved a signal failure, and so will all attempts prove which seek to provide for the work of the church by the contributions of the wealthy few. Take another illustration. What was the result of the income tax inaugurated during the war? The principle upon which it was based was to tax the larger incomes with higher rates of percentage than was levied upon the smaller incomes. It was a system of partial taxation. It was simply compelling a few to pay a special impost as a penalty for working harder, and exercising such industry and economy as enabled them to save more than their neighbors. Its influence was so injurious, and the returns so meagre, that it was soon abandoned. It did not reach the masses, and proved a false and ruinous principle in the securing of national revenue.

The great secret of the financial power of the Roman Catholic Church consists in the fact that rich and poor are alike expected to contribute of their means. In this country their members are largely, if not almost altogether, of the poorer classes, and yet their resources are surely not very limited.

Next to spirituality, the rapid growth and spread of Methodism is due to the skill manifested by John Wesley in marshaling every man, woman and child for individual work and personal endeavor. As an organizer and efficient systematizer, John Wesley is without a superior in civil, military or ecclesiastical life, and because of his organic skill and methodical workings, his followers were called *Method*-ists. Their watchword was, " Justification, sanctification, and a penny a week." It has hitherto proven itself one of the most efficient, expansive Christian institutions of modern times, and in so far as they shall become opulent and forgetful of their primitive, methodical principles and their " penny-a-week " system, shall they slacken their progressive pace and lose their evangelistic efficiency.

If we turn from the practice which has secured success to consider our duty as Christians, we shall find that there is no escaping from individual, personal responsibility in the act of giving. Each and every Christian is as much expected to use this as any and every other means of grace. Each member of every Christian family is required to contribute. After children are old enough to pray and to understand somewhat what worship is, the parents can no longer worship God, for and in the place of their children. This can be done only by each particular member of the family for himself or herself, as individually responsible to God. The wife also is expected to contribute as well as the husband. No one can worship for her. The treasury of the temple was in the court of the women, and why exclude women from this means of grace now?

As homage and worship is due to God from all creatures of his hand and care, so those who are strangers to the covenants of promise are as much bound to the observance of giving, as an act of worship, as they are bound by the commands and love of God to the observance of each and every act of obedience and worship.

The Levites gave to the priests a tithe of all the tithes they received from the people. Christ gave the didrachma, or half shekel of the sanctuary, for himself and Peter. The Apostles and first preachers of the gospel, as they freely received, did freely give. Besides these examples, there is no reason why ministers can any more dispense with this means of grace than with any other. The people are entreated to use this means of grace, and the repeated appeals to secure money for the support of objects toward which the solicitor does not of his individual means contribute alike liberally, causes irritation and engenders hostility. The pastor should *lead* the flock into the green pastures of God's blessing, and beside the still waters of his grace.

ALL are to worship God with their substance, without distinction of sex, race, rank, class, calling, condition or ability ; and whether the gift be much or little, God will determine " according to that a man hath, and not according to that he hath not "

RESULTS OF SYSTEM IN GIVING.

In presenting some of the results of system in securing the contributions of the churches, let us consider—I. The effect upon the cause, and II. The good which results to the individual contributor.

I. Let us take a church of 350 members, and let us suppose that each of these members can lay aside a fraction over three cents a day. " How many days in the week do most of us let that amount slip through our fingers without knowing whither it goes, and without feeling the outlay? We have thus twenty-five cents a week, or twelve dollars a year, from each member. This would give us, from communicants alone, $4,200 annually. Now, supposing one fifth of this number, or seventy members, can lay by fifty cents a week. This adds $910 a week. And supposing that one-twenty-fifth of this number could contribute a dollar a week. Fourteen members would thus add $364. This gives us, from communicants alone, $5,474 ; and the heaviest amount paid by any individual would be $52. When you reflect that there are those who annually contribute from three to ten times that

26

amount for the benevolent objects of the church alone, you find the amount running up very rapidly. For instance, let us say that, in addition to their $52, there are five men who give $200 a year among the various collections, and there is $1,000 more—$6,474 from the communicants only. And now we will go outside of these three hundred and fifty communicants. Let us assume that there are one hundred and fifty persons, not members of the church, who can and will give twenty-five cents a week, and we add $1,950, making a total of $8,424, and still $252 is the largest amount given by any individual.

" This estimate is made for a strong and prosperous church, and is purposely *within bounds.* The church in question could raise this amount on that simple plan, and never feel it. Any pastor, knowing the ability of his congregation, can easily make a similar computation according to the number and means of his people. And in any case he will find that the peo-people will be astonished at his figures, which will show them how a little system will enable them to double, and sometimes to treble, their contributions without feeling a burden."*

After the introduction of a regular system of week-ly offerings for benevolent purposes by the Congrega-tional churches of Providence, R. I., in writing of the results of the plan, Rev. George Harris says:

*Rev. Marvin R. Vincent, D. D., in " How Much and How to Give."

" The youngest church in Providence, the Pilgrim Church, adopted the system in 1875. In 1874 that church had contributed for all objects, $479. In 1875, by the method of weekly offerings, its contributions amounted to $1,686.97, about four times as much, and in 1876 to $2,397.97, five times as much. The Union Church adopted the system in 1873, and has the credit of introducing it. The amount given by that church the previous year was $3,540.88 ; in 1874 to the same objects, $5,064.69, and since that time the amount has increased still more. The Central Church, of which I am pastor, adopted the system in October, 1876. Our contributions during the preceding year were $3,-600 ; last year the weekly offerings amounted to $7,-674.11. The number of givers in the Union Church increased from 62 to 187, and then to 210 ; in the Central Church from 95 to to 283. This large increase of givers and of gifts has been made during a period of business depression which is almost unprecedented, and when nearly every family has suffered pecuniary loss, directly or indirectly ; yet all are ready to continue as they have begun, and even to make some addition to the amount given."

It is evident that a good system would : 1. Secure larger contributions. 2 .It would reach the one-half or two-thirds who now give nothing at all. 3. It would substitute principle for impulse. 4. It would diminish the expenses of benevolent societies by doing away with the present necessity of sending out solicitors and agents. 5. It would enable the boards and various benevolent societies to go forth in their might to accomplish the great work assigned to them.

II. The results which would come to the contributor from the faithful use of a plan of constant giving are very numerous. 1. He would enjoy all the temporal blessings which God has promised to such as are faithful stewards of his material wealth. 2. It would abate the force of avarice. 3. It would convert giving into a source of pleasure. As Mr. Peabody said to a rich man: " It is sometimes hard for one who has devoted the best part of his life to the accumulation of money to spend it for others ; but practice it and keep on practicing it, and I assure you it comes to be a pleasure." 4. It would increase the giver's means of usefulness. 5. *Systematic* giving tends to cultivate exactness and system in the transaction of business, and thus to secure success. 6. It will quicken a more earnest desire for the conversion of all men. 7. It will aid in counteracting every influence which would lead to dishonesty in business. 8. It will, if used in the right spirit, prepare the contributor for God's blessing in time and eternal happiness in heaven.

But the custom of universal worship in giving

accomplishes another grand result in addition to
increasing the facilities of the church and enlarging
her usefulness. Each contribution increases the interest of the contributor in the church and her charities.
England could pay her national debt if she desired,
but her policy is *not* to pay it. By having a national
debt a safe investment is afforded for the people, and
on account of this money invested in the government,
each and every bondholder is made to feel an abiding,
personal interest in the stability and prosperity of the
government. When a subject of the crown purchases
a portion of the national loan, it is as though he paid
his money to purchase for himself an enlarged patriot-
ism. The same principle holds true in the church.
The men who care little or nothing whether the particular church with which they are associated is built
up or torn down, are they not almost without exception of those who contribute little or nothing toward
the support of the church? They have no treasure
there, neither have they any heart there. Those who
contribute most, in proportion to their ability, purchase most interest in the success and usefulness of
the church. Augustine says: " We give earth, and
receive heaven. We give the temporal, and receive
the eternal. We give things corruptible, and receive
the immortal. Lastly, we give what God has bestowed,
and receive God himself. Let us not be slothful in

such a commerce as this.   Let us not continue poor."

ANNUAL COLLECTION PLAN.

Some congregations have such an awful sense of the local needs of their church, and such a horror of collections for general church work, that what little conscience they have left as to their duty in this matter is quieted by once a year combining the various objects into one collection, which has been aptly termed the " *omnibus* " plan.   It lessens the number of collections and diminishes the amounts to the least possible fraction.

Every pastor has heard the question, or in his work been treated as though the question were asked :

" When will this incessant begging for money cease ?   It is call upon call, now for this, now for that, and I am sick and weary of it."   More ask the question than those who put it into words.

" The answer is as easy as the question.   It will never cease.   It is a part of the law of the situation. While there remains a heathen on earth, an unfaithful Christian, a sick man, soul-sick or body-sick, an orphan child, a cripple, an outcast, a wretched creature anywhere with any wretchedness, the demands will still be made, and they will still be answered worse or better.

" When all men on earth are blessed, when the sunlight of heaven gilds the hills and valleys of the world, and wraps the blue seas in eternal calm, then may men rest from their working and their giving— not before."

Solicitors are too timid just at this point. Each cause should be presented separately and heroically, and in such a manner as to commend the cause to the favorable consideration of every honest mind and earnest heart. Let there be no shrinking back from duty, no cowardly apologies, no cold indifference. The home church is dependent upon the heathen, as much as the heathen, or any other needy cause is dependent upon them. In giving, God designs a greater blessing to rest upon the giver than upon the recipient. " It is more blessed to give than to receive." In the act of contributing God contemplates not only the building up of his kingdom in the world, but the building up of his kingdom in the heart of the individual contributor as well. The churches which live only for themselves, regardless of others, invariably decline, while those which reach out a help- ing hand to save others, save themselves. It is stated that "fifty years ago thirty Baptist churches in the State of Maryland declared themselves opposed to missions, while two alone stood in favor of them. The two increased to thousands, while the anti-mission churches dwindled away till they now number not more than seven or eight persons." How often we see the Scripture verified : " There is that scattereth, and yet increaseth ; and there is that withholdeth more than is meet, but it tendeth to poverty."

ANNUAL SUBSCRIPTION.

The annual subscription is a modification of the annual collection plan. Annually the subscription is circulated among the congregation on Sabbath, or a solicitor goes from house to house during the week. These subscriptions are placed into a common fund, and then apportioned by the pastor, or council, to the various objects. This putting all benevolent objects together, and then attempting to do the work of an entire year 'n a single act, is as absurd as it would be to take the bread, and meat, and potatoes, and all the other food required for an entire year, and placing it all together, attempt to eat it at a single meal.

The disadvantages of this method, or want of method, are evident :

1. It is inadequate in the amounts which it secures. If the church will repent of its sin and return to the ordained law of the *tithe*, the condition of the whole world will be revolutionized. The discovery of the law of gravitation, or of electricity, or the application of the power of steam, or the laws of sound—none of these, nor all of them combined, have wrought greater changes in philosophy, or in the physical condition of man, than would be wrought in the life, energy and

efficiency of the church and the spiritual condition of the world, by a return to God's methods for the accomplishment of God's work.

2. It allows selfishness and covetousness to acquire overmastering strength. Constant giving tends to abate the force of avarice, but these annual plans nourish the besetting sin of the church, and give to " *covetousness,* WHICH IS IDOLATRY," the seal of orthodoxy and respectability.

3. It affords no opportunity for presenting the great causes of the church and awakening in the minds and hearts of the people that interest which will enlist their prayers for God's blessing upon the objects toward which they are asked to contribute.

QUARTERLY COLLECTION PLAN.

The quarterly collection is a great improvement upon the annual method, but it lacks that element of *frequency* which would enable it to bring the church up to its standard of duty and privilege in giving. If some cause is to be presented quarterly, and simply a basket collection is to be taken, the system has numerous defects. Some will absent themselves, and others will be unavoidably absent when the collection is taken. Stormy weather, sickness, absence from home on the part of members, and other causes, will have a damaging effect upon the collection. If the cause be missions, and the day be pleasant, and the house full,

27

under the inspiration of the occasion and subject, the pastor " may talk so long that some would lose interest and give scarcely anything. Some may have sustained losses during the week, which make them feel poor on that particular Sunday, while on another Sunday, after a prosperous week, they would feel generous ; one has left his pocketbook at home ; another has forgotten to bring money." These and other difficulties have to be met.

A QUARTERLY SUBSCRIPTION PLAN.

We append a plan which has overcome many of the difficulties of the usual quarterly basket collection.

On the Sabbath appointed let the envelopes be placed in each seat, or distributed by the deacons or a committee, to each family or part of a family represented in the congregation, not omitting any visitors. The form of the envelope may be suggested by the following :

" They shall not appear before the Lord empty; every man shall give as he is able."—*Deut. xvi. 16, 17.*

BENEFICENCE.

" Lay up for yourselves treasures in heaven."—*Matt. vi. 20.*

" To do good and to communicate, forget not."—*Heb. xiii. 16.*

RETURN THIS ENVELOPE NEXT SABBATH.

The envelope should contain a card like the following, or the same may be printed entire on one side of a slip of heavy paper :

(CARD.)

_____

FOR BENEVOLENT PURPOSES.

" Honor the Lord with thy substance and with the first-fruits of all thine increase."---*Prov. iii. 9.*

	$	Cts.
(See Other Side.) Total.		

(REVERSE SIDE OF CARD.)

Take this card home, and during the week prayerfully consider the claims of the cause presented in the accompanying tract. Let every member of the family, in the spirit of Christian liberality, subscribe something, and whether it be much or little, God will determine "according to that a man hath, and not according to that he hath not." When all have subscribed, add up the amount, place this card, together with the money, in the envelope, seal and return next Sabbath.

The cards are not to be inspected by others, but the pastor will keep a complete record of all contributions, and admonish such delinquents as neglect or but partially use this means of Christian growth in grace.

"There is that scattereth, and yet increaseth; and there is that withholdeth more than is meet, but it tendeth to poverty."—*Prov. xi.* 24.

The envelope and cards are suited to any collection, but the accompanying tract should set forth the cause for which the collection is asked. The tract should be brief, like the following:

(TRACT.)

THE COLLECTION NEXT SABBATH.

The Education of Ministers.

One of the regular objects toward which the General Synod asks its members to contribute is in aiding young men in the very important work of preparing for the gospel ministry. To say nothing of the ever increasing demand for ministers, it is necessary that a goodly number should continually be preparing to take the places of the 55,000 ministers who are yearly giving their lives in the preaching of the gospel. In the single year of 1879, 31 Lutheran ministers died in the United States. The average age of these was 56 years. Taking this as a fair index of ministerial longevity, 2,115 ministers would be necessary annually to take the places made vacant by death and infirmity. It is but right that the people for whose spiritual and eternal good this great army of Christian ministers are using their talents and giving their lives should assist the needy young men who are being fitted in mind and heart to fill the places made vacant by death and superannuation.

Many of these young men are poor, and without our aid would never be able to enter the sacred office to which they feel that God has called them. By withholding from them the already insufficient stipend, the church would be cutting off the very hands which are to feed and minister to her. Let us not be deceived; these young men and the church are mutually dependent. *Each* needs the help of the other. The benefaction is not all on one side.

Shall Christ say to you, and to each member of your family : " Verily I say unto you, inasmuch as ve have done it unto one of the least of these, my brethren, ye have done it unto me ?"

On the Sabbath that the envelopes are distributed, a large card, printed in large, clear type, should be suspended in front of the pulpit.

(CARD.)

BENEVOLENT CONTRIBUTIONS

NEXT

LORD'S DAY.

The following Sabbath, when the envelopes are returned, lest any may have forgotten the collection or left their envelopes at home, extra envelopes should be left in the seats or in a convenient place, and the following card suspended in front of the pulpit :

(CARD.)

BENEVOLENT CONTRIBUTIONS

TO-DAY.

These cards should be *not less* than two feet long by fourteen inches broad, or one card may be made to serve the double purpose by having it printed upon both sides.

This system is also well suited to be used monthly. All that is necessary is to change the tract to suit the object, the envelopes and cards being the same for all objects.

Advantages.—The advantages of this plan are : (*a.*) It secures a subscription instead of a basket collection, and that without any delaying of the congregation after service. (*b.*) It secures thoughtful, intelligent giving, as it affords a means of knowing the needs of the cause, and gives an entire week to consider the subject and decide upon the amount to contribute. (*c.*) Each member of the family is requested and expected to subscribe something, and this exercises and disciplines the young in this grace also. (*d.*) It enables the session, or the pastor, to know just how each member of the church is discharging this Christian duty. (*e.*) It affords a means of knowing who the absentees are, so that if desirable they may be called upon privately. (*f.*) The greatest thing to be said in its favor is that it has succeeded wherever faithfully tried.*

MONTHLY CONTRIBUTION PLANS.

The superior principles of the monthly plan, after what has been said on the foregoing plans, requires no comment. We append a number of forms and methods :

---

*The cards and envelopes, printed and ready for use, may be had of I. K. Funk & Co.

A Circular Letter.—The method of sending out a circular letter at the beginning of the year setting forth the needs of each board and asking for a subscription which shall be paid monthly has proven successful in many churches.

One form of circular letter, after presenting the claims of the various boards, contains the following blank :

I will Contribute Monthly for

Foreign Missions,   -   -   - $

Home Missions, -   -   -   -

Beneficiary Education,   -   -

Church Extension.   -   -   -

Pastor's Fund,   -   -   -

    Name

    Address

Please fill out the above and send it to the Pastor at as early a date as possible.

Another Form.

ANNUAL CIRCULAR.

PLAN OF

SYSTEMATIC CONTRIBUTION

OF THE

First Presbyterian Church, of Trenton, N. J.

This paper is to be retained by the Subscriber.

TIME.	OBJECT.	AMOUNT.
1st Sabbath in Jan.	Board of Foreign Missions.	
3d " " "	Deacons' Fund.	
1st " " Feb.	The Commissioners' and Contingent Fund of the General Assembly, and the Session Fund of this Church.	
1st " " Mar.	Board of Education.	
1st " " April.	State Mission Fund.	
3d " " "	Deacons' Fund.	
1st " " May.	Board of Publication.	
1st " " June.	Sunday-schools.	
1st " " July.	Board of Church Extension.	
3d " " "	Deacons' Fund.	
1st " " August.	Freedmen's Fund.	
1st " " Sept.	Disabled Ministers.	
1st " " Oct.		
3d " " "	Deacons' Fund.	
1st " " Nov.	Domestic Missions.	
1st " " Dec.	Bible Society.	

Contributors can send their money to the Treasurer of Session if they have not deposited it in the collection box.

THIS DUPLICATE To be cut off and Deposited in the COLLECTION BOX

OBJECT.													
For Missions.	Deacons' Fund.	Three Funds.	Education.	State Missions.	Deacons' Fund.	Publication.	Sunday-schools.	Church Extension.	Deacons' Fund.	Freedmen's Fund.	Disabled Ministers.	Deacons' Fund.	Domestic Missions. Bible Society.

AMOUNT.

(REVERSE SIDE OF CIRCULAR.)

The object of the *Board of Foreign Missions* is to send the gospel to the foreign world and to the Indian tribes within our own territories.

That of the *Board of Education* is to aid poor and pious young men in obtaining an education with a view to the ministry, and to aid in the religious instruction of our children and youth.

The *State Mission Fund* is intended to meet the calls of Presbytery for assissance to mission churches within the bounds of the state.

That of the *Board of Publication* is to print and circulate throughout the country a sound and healthful religious literature.

That of the *Church Extension Committee* is to aid in the erection of Presbyterian church edifices throughout the country.

That of the *Freedmen's Fund* is to sustain missions among the freedmen.

The *Fund for Disabled Ministers, &c.,* is disbursed by a committee of the Trustees of the General Assembly, to aid disabled ministers of our church who are in want, and the needy widows and orphans of our deceased ministers.

That of the *Board of Domestic Missions* is to send the gospel to the destitute regions of our own country, and to aid in sustaining our feeble churches.

28

Suggestive Figures.—Where it is desired to raise a fixed amount for benevolence it is very desirable that the pastoral letter should contain some suggestive figures which will enable the people to see how the work can be done, and also to aid them in arriving at their duty in the matter. Let us suppose that with a congregation of 615 members, it is desired to raise $10,000 or $12,000 for benevolent work. This amount will startle most of the members, and yet the following table will render the problem quite a simple one:

5 persons giving $5.00	each amounts to	$25.00 per week ;	or,	$1,3c0 per year.
10	"	3.00	"	"	30.00	"	"	1,560	"
20	"	2 00	"	"	40.00	"	"	2,080	"
30	"	1.00	"	"	30.00	"	"	1,560	"
50	"	.50	"	"	25.00	"	"	1,300	"
100	"	.25	"	"	25.00	"	"	1,300	"
150	"	.20	"	"	30.00	"	"	1,560	"
200	"	.10	"	"	20.00	"	"	1,040	"
50	"	.05	"	"	2.50	"	"	130	"

615 $11,830

Schedule of Monthly Collections.—In some churches a printed schedule of collections is tacked up in the front of each pew:

SPECIAL COLLECTIONS
ON THE LAST SUNDAY IN EACH MONTH.

1881.

January, - - Foreign Missions.

February, - Diocesan Missions.

March, - - Orphan Asylum.

April, - - Aged and Infirm Clergy Fund.

May, - - Parish Sunday-schools.

June, -	-	Diocesan Convention Fund.
July,	-	Religious Publications.
August,	-	Diocesan Missions.
September, -	-	Bishop's Salary.
October,-	-	Theological Education.
November, -	-	Domestic Missions.
December,	-	Parish Library.

" Remember the Lord thy God, for it is He that giveth thee power to get wealth "—*Deut. viii. 18.*

Or the year may be divided into sections, "appropriating to each board as many consecutive Sabbaths as its comparative importance seems to demand, and appropriating all the sums received within this period to it. This gives a specific time to each board, and affords the opportunity to the pastor for stating the objects, operations and wants of each scheme of the church."

WEEKLY CONTRIBUTION PLANS.

The weekly contribution method, connecting the offertory with each public service, possesses many excellent features. " When, in 1842, the Free Church of Scotland was by a quick stroke cut off from governmental support, and had at once to provide for church buildings, manses, salaries, schools, colleges, the poor, church extension at home, foreign missions and all, it did so by returning to a system of weekly offerings."

(*a.* It makes giving a part of the regular worship of the sanctuary. "They shall not appear before the Lord empty; every man shall give as he is able." (*b.*) It is frequent, and crystallizes impulse into principle. (*c.*) It reaches all who attend upon divine worship. It is far better for the churches, and the cause of religion, to have five hundred dollars paid by one or two hundred persons, than to have the same amount paid by one or two wealthy individuals, or even by twenty or thirty. It is not simply to secure the people's money, but to render the people more unselfish and more like Him, who gave even himself for us. (*d.*) It exercises the people in a Christian grace. The apostle says: "See that ye abound in this grace also."

A Basket Collection.--The following plan has been in successful operation in the Shady Side Presbyterian Church, of Pittsburg:

"A contribution for the benevolent work of the church is taken every Sabbath morning. From these funds the following specified amounts are deducted, viz.: For the support of the Sabbath-school, $12.50 per month; for the 'Commissioners' and Contingent Fund of the General Assembly,' the Sessional and Deacons' Fund of our own church, $25 per month, and for the support of missions within the bounds of our own city and Presbytery, from $8 to $12 per month, at the discretion of the session. The balance of the funds are distributed monthly to the several boards and committees having charge of the benevolent work of the church, under the General Assembly, on the basis of the following schedule:

Foreign Missions.....................25 per cent.
Home Missions....................20 "
Sustentation.......................10 "
Education.........................10 "
Church erection....................10 "
Freedmen.........................10 "
Publication....................... 5 "
Ministerial Relief..................10 "

"The session reserves the right to set apart any Sabbath for the purpose of taking a collection for any special object they may deem proper—the congregation always to be notified in advance of said purpose. Any person desiring to contribute directly, or to make a special contribution to any object, whether in the above list or not, is permitted to do so by accompanying their contributions with a card, indicating their wish."

The pastor, Rev. William T. Beatty, says of it: " The above plan has more than met the expectations of the congregation; it has secured larger contributions than we ever realized before; it has been less burdensome; it has given every opportunity for the presentation of the claims of the boards, and it has supplied a fund from which the officers of the church can meet the assessments of the higher judications, and from which they can draw for such other expenses as are legitimate, without the necessity of a separate appeal, or a special collection."

As congregations ought to know not only the needs of any object, but also what they are giving to aid it, it is suggested to pastors that they should publicly state the amount received on the Sabbath following a collection, so as to satisfy a desire for information, to stimulate benevolence, and to afford matter for prayer, humility and thankfulness. Also, that, before every public collection, blank cards and pencils be placed in every pew for the use of those not prepared with money. *A collection is often doubled in amount by this simple precaution.* At the public collections for the several boards a much larger amount than usual can often be raised by giving the congregation a definite object to accomplish. State how much is desired for the object.

An Envelope Plan.—In 1873 an envelope system of weekly offerings was introduced into the Congregational churches of Providence, R. I., which secured the most satisfactory results. We present the plan as given by Rev. George Harris in the *Congregationalist* in November, 1877 :

(CARD)

BENEVOLENT OFFERINGS

OF THE

CENTRAL

CONGREGATIONAL CHURCH AND CONGREGATION,

PROVIDENCE.

$ .01 | PLEASE mark with an ' in the column on
.02 the left the sum you are willing to pledge as a
.03 weekly offering to the Lord, for the year begin-
.04 ning October 1, 1876 (using a blank space if
.05 you select a sum not mentioned).

Write your name and residence at the bottom of this card, and deposit it in the contri-
.10 bution box on the following Sabbath.
.15 A package of small envelopes will then be
.20 furnished you (one for each week.
.25 Each Lord's day enclose the amount of your
.30 weekly offering in the envelope which bears
that date, and place it sealed in one of the
boxes at the doors of the church.
.50 In case of absence for one or more Sundays,
enclose the whole amount due with the next
offering that is made, and destroy the enve-
1.00 lopes that have not been used.

This pledge being purely voluntary. may be
recalled at any time by giving notice to the
2.00 COMMITTEE.

5.00 *Name*

10.00 *Residence*

(CARD, REVERSE SIDE.)

$	1. *Foreign Missions.*
$	2. *Home Missions.*
$	3. *American Missionary Association.* For Freedmen.
$	4. *Cause of Education.*
$	5. *Sabbath-school.*
$	6. *Woman's Board of Foreign Missions.*
$	7.
$	8.
$	9. *General Fund.*
$	

Please indicate how you wish the sum total of your offerings for the year to be divided, by marking above against the names of such objects as you may select the amount you wish to give to each. The sum total of your offerings for the year will be 52 times your weekly donation.

All gifts not otherwise designated will go into the General Fund, to be disposed of by vote of the Standing Committee of the church.

Gifts designed for any special object, and marked with the name of the object, can be placed in the boxes at the door (with or without donor's name), and will be forwarded to their destination.

This system of weekly offerings has been adopted by the church, and the hearty co-operation of all members of the congregation, both young and old, is cordially invited.

Each one is given " a box containing fifty-two small envelopes, dated October 1, October 8, October 15, and so on to the end of the year. Every Sunday he encloses the amount he has pledged and drops it into the box as he enters the church. If he has been absent, the envelopes tell their own story ; he sees that some have not been used, and encloses the whole amount due in the envelope for the day.

" This system secures the small gifts of a congregation, and swells them into a large volume. For nine persons in ten it is easier to give twenty-five cents a week than to give thirteen dollars once a year—it is easier to give a dollar every week than to give fifty-two dollars at one time. How much do you think the contributions of five cents a week amounted to in my church last year ? Fifty-eight persons gave five cents a week, and the sum total was $153.70. If one should go out to get $153 from gifts of only five cents, he would say I do not know people enough to give it. Fifty persons gave ten cents each every week, and the sum total of their offerings was $265—two hundred and sixty-five dollars in ten-cent pieces. Thirty-three persons gave twenty-five cents each week, and together gave $437.25, and the entire amount given in sums ranging from one cent to twenty-five cents was $1,119.84. Thirty-two persons gave fifty cents each week, and their total was $848. Fourteen persons

29

gave one dollar each week, and together contributed $742, while the whole amount in sums of from one cent to one dollar a week was $3,094.14, and was given by 262 of the 283 givers. Those who gave more than one dollar a week were our large givers before, although their gifts increased under the new system; but I have very little doubt that nine-tenths of the $3,000 was clear gain; that but very little of it would have been gathered into occasional collections. Here is a weighty argument in favor of the weekly system, and although some of the givers made sacrifices, it is likely that the great majority were scarcely aware that they had given anything. A capital mistake in our ordinary methods is that the few give and not the many; while the large streams of benevolence flow, the small rills are not kept open. Those who, by a small gift each week, might contribute a fine sum in a year, practically give nothing. It is apparently not worth while for collectors to visit those who can give but a few cents, or if they should, shame or pride would keep many from putting down their names for a small sum."

For an envelope system uniting the current expenses of the church with the benevolent contributions, see the Bellefonte Method, page 146.

Another Form.—Some persons may like the following form, beginning it with a dedication or pledge:

FORM OF DEDICATION.

After due deliberation and prayer, I do hereby record the resolution I have made, to lay up the sum of .... weekly, to be expended on religious and benevolent objects. Out of this sum I have determined to give to the under mentioned objects the amount attached to each.

(Signed)

——————1880. A. B. C.——————.

	$	CTS.
For the Support of my Pastor...........		
For the Poor of my Church.............		
For the Bible Society.................		
For Foreign Missions...............		
For Domestic Missions.................		
For Board of Education................		
For Sabbath-school Purposes...........		
For Board of Publication..............		
For Church Extension.................		
For Widow's Fund..................		

Weekly Offerings (Gathered Monthly.)—Weekly offerings may be indicated upon a card and placed in an envelope to be gathered monthly by collectors, who shall meet together to report and pay the money to the general treasurer. For convenience, the congregation may be divided into sections. While making collections, the committee should at the same time distribute the cards and envelopes for the ensuing month. The reverse side of the card, given below, should present in brief the object of the various funds for which money is solicited:

(CARD.)

"Lay up for yourselves treasures in heaven."—*Matt. vi. 20.*

"To do good, and to communicate, forget not."—*Heb. xiii. 19.*

"Trust not in uncertain riches, but in the living God."—*1 Tim. vi. 17.*

"Remember the Lord thy God, for it is He that giveth thee power to get wealth."—*Deut. viii. 18.*

"Freely ye have received, freely give."—*Matt. x. 8.*

"Every man according as he purposeth in his heart, so let him give; not grudgingly, or of necessity; for God loveth a cheerful giver."—*2 Cor. ix. 7.*

	Lord's Day's of a Month.					TOATL.
	1	2	3	4	5	
Foreign Missions.						
Domestic Missions.						
Education.						
Publication.						
Church Extension.						
Disabled Ministers.						
Freedmen.						
Sabbath-school.						
Poor.						
Sessional Fund.						
Total.						

(ENVELOPE, FOR CARD AND CONTRIBUTION.)

GIFTS FOR THE TREASURY OF THE LORD

ON THE

FIRST DAY OF THE WEEK.

Presbyterian Church, Buffalo, N. Y.

☞To be called for at the close of the month.

PLANS FOR DAILY OFFERINGS.

During the past few years a system has been in successful operation in many of the Presbyterian congregations, which is known as the

Foundation-Fund Plan.—The plan is this: (*a.*) Each communicant who is willing to contribute *at least* a cent a day, each day in the year, is enrolled and called upon monthly; also, all attendants, who are not members, and children. (*b.*) The congregation is districted, and fifteen contributors assigned to each collector. (*c.*) The collectors, who are usually the Christian women of the church, act under the direction of the pastor, or a special treasurer appointed by the session, and collect, report and pay over the money monthly. (*d.*) The total amount collected is apportioned to the various boards by the session. (*e.*) The regular stated collections on the Sabbath are taken up as usual, thus affording an opportunity to all who are able to contribute more than at the " foundation rate " of one cent a day.

The plan has some special advantages: (*a.*) It reaches every communicant. It is not, however, asked as a tax, but as a means of constant exercise in the grace of giving. (*b.*) It secures in each congregation mutual acquaintance and visitation, and brings to notice worthy cases of want or sickness. (*c.*) It secures a large increase of benevolent funds, and keeps the people constantly in sympathy with the great agencies of the church. (*d.*) It is flexible, being capable of a change in the definite amount contributed daily, the mode of collecting and the reception of extra offerings by the collectors, without disturbing the principle which lays at the foundation of the plan.

This plan needs an efficient person to supervise and instruct the collectors, and one who will devote to it the time and perseverance necessary to render any plan a decided success.

DIRECTIONS TO COLLECTORS.

1. Collect in the first week for each month, at the rate of one cent a day, and mark the *amount paid* in the proper column.

2. If any one wishes to give more than at the rate of one cent a day, make a memorandum of such *additional sums* on the page provided for them, and place the total amount of these sums for the month on the line marked Miscellaneous.

3. If for any reason it is *necessary* to receive for more than one month in advance, mark the amount paid in the column of the month for which you are collecting, and cross the columns of the succeeding full months paid for, thus —. Any balance less than a full month, credit to Miscelloneous, the same as with sums over the foundation rate.

4. Enclose the total amount in the printed envelope, and return to the treasurer monthly at such time and place as he shall direct, with such written remarks as may be needed for his information.

(COLLECTOR'S CARD.)

No.	NAME.	District No. JANUARY. Collect 31 cts.	FEBRUARY. Collect 28 cts.	MARCH. Collect 31 cts.	APRIL. Collect 30 cts.	MAY. Collect 31 cts.	JUNE. Collect 30 cts.	JULY. Collect 31 cts.
1								
2								
3								
4								
5								
6								
7								
8								
9								
10								
11								
12								
13								
14								
15								
	Miscellaneous Gifts.							
	TOTAL . . .							

(COLLECTOR'S CARD.)

AUGUST.	SEPTEMBER.	OCTOBER.	NOVEMBER.	DECEMBER.	TOTAL.	RESIDENCE.	
						No.	STREET.
Collect 31 cts.	Collect 30 cts.	Collect 31 cts.	Collect 30 cts.	Collect 31 cts.			

30

Collector's Memorandum of Miscellaneous Gifts.

Jan.	Feb.	Mar.	April.	May.	June.
TOTAL.					

July.	Aug.	Sept.	Oct.	Nov.	Dec.
TOTAL.					

FORM OF ENVELOPE FOR COLLECTORS.

Rec'd from No.	Dolls.	Cts.	REMARKS.
1			
2			
3			
4			
5			
6			
7			
8			
9			
10			
11			
12			
13			
14			
15			
Misc.			
TOTAL,			ENCLOSED AND SEALED.

Collector's Report for Month of _____

District No. _____

_____ *Collector.*

Another Plan.

Rev. Herman S. Cook, pastor of the Lutheran Church of Lyonville, Penn'a, has met with more than ordinary success in raising money for benevolent work. Concerning his method he writes :

"By earnest, patient, personal effort we have introduced a system of contributing to the benevolent agencies of the church which has resulted in greatly developing this important branch of church work. Each member of the church, male or female, old or young, rich or poor, is requested to give something *every day* to the cause of Christ—a definite sum, if it be but one cent, or more, or less. One or two cents a day are much more easily and readily paid than $3.65 or $7.30 a year, and daily blessings call for a daily thank offering to God. On the first Sunday of every month the contributions for the month just closed are handed in in envelopes, sealed, numbered and dated, and a complete record kept of the contributions of each member In this way almost every member is reached, and contributes frequently, regularly, deliberately, and we trust prayerfully, as the Lord has prospered him or her. Before this system was introduced the contributions of the Lyonville congregation aggregated from $100 to $150 a year. The system has now been in operation almost two years, and during the last twelve months has resulted in an average contribution of $24.60 per month, an aggregate of $295.37 for the year, an average annual contribution of $3.28 per member. This in a country congregation of ninety members, of only average wealth, at a time when their home expenses were largely increased by extensive repairs to their church, and they had also during the year liberally contributed to the endow-ment fund of Pennsylvania College.

" We believe this system to be one of the very best, and sufficiently flexible to be adapted to any people under any circumstances."

THE BOX SYSTEM.

Some years ago a box system was introduced among the churches of the General Synod of the Lutheran church. It consisted of a neat little box with an opening, into which a regular offering was to be placed each Sabbath morning. The boxes were returned quarterly to the pastor or committee, and the con-tents given consecutively to Foreign Missions, Home Missions, Church Extension and Beneficiary Educa-tion. After removing the contents, the opening in the bottom of the box was again sealed and returned to the owner, whose name was indicated by the number of the box. They were neatly gotten up, adorned with appropriate Scripture passages, and for a few years did efficient service.

CONTRIBUTION BOXES AT THE CHURCH DOOR.

In some churches contribution boxes are put up in conspicuous places, at the end of each aisle, or at the church door. These are for contributions to special objects, which are designated upon a card tacked in the front of each pew, or stated from the pulpit before dismissing the congregation. This plan is more generally used by congregations where large numbers of strangers congregate for worship each Sabbath, as at Spurgeon's church, in London, England, and others in this country. These boxes are used generally in connection with the regular basket collections.

PRIVATE TREASURY FOR OFFERINGS.

The most liberal and at the same time the most cheerful contributors are those who statedly lay aside into a private treasury that portion which they design for the support of the gospel and benevolent purposes. The most cheerful contributor we have ever had among our own people was one who kept a purse, which he called the Lord's purse, into which at regular and frequent intervals he placed a part of his income for benevolent purposes. No worthy cause was turned away empty. Each member of his family were life members of the American Bible Society ; every one who labored for him were made life members of the County Bible Society, and in like manner he contributed to all benevolent objects. It is really refreshing to meet such men. Rev. L. A. Gotwald, D. D., in writing of one with whom he had been associated in a former charge, says:

" I often asked him for contributions toward various benevolent objects, and was never rebuffed nor refused, his only question ever being, 'How much *ought* I to give?' Sitting with him in his office one day, and conversing on this subject of benevolence, I said in substance to him: 'Mr. W., I often ask you for money for religious and charitable purposes, and you always give, and give liberally. May I ask you how you manage to be able always to do so? Have you a plan or system in your beneficence?' Turning in his chair, and pointing to one corner of the room, he said to me: 'Do you see that safe? In that safe is a secret drawer. The drawer is marked ' *The Lord's Drawer.*' Into that drawer, at the end of each week, I deposit, as nearly as I can estimate it correctly, the one-tenth of all that I have made during that week. I do this as regularly and systematically as I attend to any other business transaction—for that I regard also as business, my business with the Lord. Having once thus deposited money in that drawer, I then regard that money as no longer in any sense mine. It is the Lord's. I am simply the custodian and disposer of it. And hence when you, or any other of the Lord's accredited agents call upon me, and say that the Lord sent you here for some of his money in my hands, it is the easiest thing in the world, and a real pleasant thing also, to go right there to that drawer, and pay out to the Lord his own money—not mine, but his. *That*, sir, is my plan, and *that* is how I always have something to give. How much did you say you wanted to-day?' "

Surely no better method could be devised which will enable the contributor to give " heartily as unto the Lord."

PLEDGE OR COVENANT.

" The biography of eminently pious and useful men since the Reformation shows that great numbers of them have rec gnized the obligation statedly to devote a portion of their income to charitable uses. Lord Chief Justice Hale, Rev. Dr. Hammond, Baxter, Doddridge and others rugularly gave a tenth; Dr. Watts, a fifth; Mrs. Rowe, one-half. Rev. John Wesley, when his income was thirty pounds, lived on twenty-eight and gave two, and when his income rose to sixty pounds, and afterwards to one hundred and twenty, he still lived on twenty-eight, and gave all the remainder. Mr. Nathaniel R. Cobb, a merchant connected with the Baptist church in Boston, in 1821, at the age of twenty-three, drew up and subscribed the following covenant, to which he faithfully adhered till on his deathbed he praised God that by acting according to it he had given in charity more than $40,000 :"

" By the grace of God, I will never be worth more than $50,000.

" By the grace of God, I will give one-fourth of the net profits of my business to charitable and religious uses.

" If I am ever worth $20,000, I will give one-half of my net profits ; and if I am ever worth $30,000, I will give three-fourths, and the whole, after $50,000. So help me God, or give to a more faithful steward, and set me aside. . N. R. COBB."

Another Form.

Knowing that all things come of Thee, O Lord, and acknowledging my obligation to devote at least one-tenth of all my increase to religious purposes, I hereby prayerfully, deliberately and cheerfully covenant, as Jacob of old, that " of all that Thou shalt give me, I will surely give the tenth to Thee."

.   *Name*

Date .

We appeal to all Christians to adopt some method by which they may accurately ascertain the amount of their income, and then religiously to devote at least one-tenth to sacred uses. " This is the rent which reminds the tenant that he is not owner in fee ; this is the interest which reminds the borrower that the principal belongs not to him ; this is the tribute-money

31

which reminds a subject nation that it is not independent ; this is God's share to remind his creatures that
all belongs to him." We are simply stewards, and at
the last we must render an account of our stewardship.

One thing is certain ; we must either do more, or
stop pretending to pray for the conversion of the heathen. Our gifts do not prove the sincerity of our
prayers. We should come with our hearts near our
lips, and lay our wealth at Jesus' feet. Let us not be
like the farmer who, with cribs filled with corn, was
accustomed to pray that the wants of the needy might
be supplied ; but when any one in needy circumstances
asked for a little of his corn, he said he had none to
spare. One day, after hearing his father pray for the
poor and needy, his little son said to him : " Father, I
wish I had your corn." " Why, my son, what could
you do with it ?" asked the father. The child replied,
" I would answer your prayers." The theology of the
child was eminently practical. " One of the most
common reasons why prayers are not answered is
because the life is not in harmony with the prayer.
Prayer is too frequently offered as a substitute for
neglected duty. If we pray for the conversion of the
heathen and unsaved, and yet send them not the mes-
sage of life, this prayer is unacceptable and unavailing
with God. Yet such prayers are very common. It is

one of the greatest evils in the church. It costs less sacrifice to offer earnest prayer than to do self-denying work. It is when the tithes are brought into the storehouse that God promises to pour out a blessing that there shall not be room enough to receive. The reason of prayer being unanswered is always to be found with the suppliant, and never with the Great Giver of all good, who is ever nigh unto all them that call upon him—to all that call upon him in truth."

CONCLUSION.

Christ's last command to the church is, " Go ye into all the world and preach the gospel to every creature." Have we done it? Are we doing it? In the years past the church failed to do her duty in this respect, and He who said, " Behold, I have set before thee an open door, and no man can shut it," came in His might and closed the door. One port after another was closed to missionary effort. All human endeavor was vain. " He that hath the key of David," " He that shutteth and no man openeth," had shut the door. The church was like Israel's doubting hosts. One day God opens Canaan to them—they do not enter; the next day when they would enter the door is shut, the cloud moves not, the ark of the covenant accompanies them not, they go up essaying to enter, only to turn back falling before the foe. So has the church been turned back from the lands which have

been promised to her as clearly as Canaan was promised to Israel. But now, after long years, God has
again opened the door. Again Christ is saying to the
churches, that if he be lifted up he will draw all men
unto him. If the church will enter now, no obstacle
can impede her progress. No power upon earth is
strong enough to close the door. Glorious success
awaits the cause of Christ. This is the auspicious
" to-day " in the cycles of God's all-wise providence.
No longer let the myriad mites which make the mighty
millions be lost for want of proper and necessary system. Restore the offertory to its appointed place in
the family, the Sunday-school and the church. Never
did the precious opportunities which God opens call
more imperatively for the adoption of such measures as
will secure scriptural beneficence among all classes.

CHAPTER VII.

THE SABBATH COLLECTION.

It is really not surprising that the basket collections at the regular service on the Sabbath should
amount, as they generally do, to comparatively
nothing at all. " Alexander the Coppersmith " has
done the collection much evil too, and yet again and
again we hear this essential part of worship stigmatized, and belittled, and profaned, and made despica-
ble by calling it the " *Penny Collection.*" That name
alone is enough to kill it. A man who speaks of the
gathering of the offerings of the people as the " taking
of a penny collection " is guilty of sacrilege. It is
speaking irreverently of that which is as sacred as any

other part of the worship of the sanctuary. Under the Jewish system no worship was complete without a gift, and the act of giving was itself an act of worship. When David and the princes of Israel assembled to make an offering for the building of the temple, their prayers and offerings ascended to heaven together, and when Solomon dedicated that temple his great prayer and great offering, of twenty and two thousand oxen and an hundred and twenty thousand sheep, came up in gratitude together before God. Now, however, this essential part of worship is not only slighted, or treated with disrespect, but some have even ejected the offertory from the house of God Nor are they content with their sacrilege, but proclaim their shame in the public print by concluding their " religious notices " with the announcement of " no collection." Oh, what a relief to the worshipers to be permitted worship an entire hour, consoled by the sublime thought that at the close they are not to be annoyed by a collection or have their devotions disturbed by the jingling of money on the plates. Any minister who ejects the offertory from the sanctuary is guilty of sacrilege, and if he proclaims it, is guilty of heresy, and if he were expelled from the sacred office of the ministry would only receive what his conduct so justly merits.

This course is the result of a desire to gratify the

wishes of a sordid, stingy, covetous few, who know nothing of the grace of giving. Martin Luther said that a man had to be converted three times; first his head, then his heart, and then his pocketbook. To say the least, these people need the third conversion, and might be much improved by a little more of the other two. When professing Christians find themselves getting so near heaven during the sermon that they cannot get back in time for the collection, they may safely regard themselves as deluded—the difficult *up*-hill work attests the direction with great suggestiveness.

Another reason why the collection is not a success is the manner in which the offerings are gathered. The collectors catch the general infection, and, as if they were ashamed of their business, go hurrying from pew to pew, presenting the basket in an irreverent manner, and as if to say, " this is no part of the service ; it is only a penny collection, and nothing is expected from most of you."

In speaking of the offertory, and presenting its use as a lost act of worship, Rev. Hugh Miller Thompson, D. D., says :

" It is another of the cases where our theories shame our practice, where our professions put our actions to the blush, that the offertory has become, in our worship, almost an impertinence. Our people do not understand its meaning. Our clergy too often do not dare, if they know it themselves, to make the people know it.

" Men are to be taught that giving to the Lord is an essential part of public worship, quite as essential as singing or praying. They are to be instructed in the plain truth that words must go out in deeds. They must recognize the alms-basin as an essential part of church furniture, the putting of money into it as a devotional act. Their special attention must be called to the name by which their contributions, given in church, are called in the plain English of the Prayer Book ' the devotions of the people.'

" The whole duty of giving has grown dim, the sense of responsibility for wealth dead, in the minds of men. The Lord's treasury is like a beggar's dish. The clergy have grown cowardly about this part of Christian duty. When they urge it, it is with half arguments and cowardly compromises. They have a feeling that it almost degrades them to " dun for paltry money," for even a good cause. So highly ' spiritual ' have we all become, that our religion must not even name filthy lucre.

" Meanwhile, there stands that solemn service of the offertory, clear, bold, uncompromising, making giving a solemn act of religion ; calling the offered thing by its old name, a ' devotion ;' bringing forward this act of piety in the forefront of the most solemn religious service of the church of God ; asking its performance as repentance and faith are asked—for a preparation for the worthy reception of Christ's body and blood.

" In these days we know no doctrine of primitive Christianity which needs reviving more than this doctrine of the offertory ; no teaching which is more needed by the men of the time than the emphatic teaching of that most ancient and primitive institution.

" Men need to be taught that they bring their whole lives to church with them, that they do not drop at the door the stains of the market and the 'Change. They require to have it pressed home that the gains which cannot be consecrated to the Lord are gains which are ' the price of blood,' the blood of their own souls. They want the truth that God holds them responsible for every bargain and speculation, and that all the singing and praying in the world will not make an unjust profit other than a curse. They are to know that every day is a God's service or a devil's service, and that two hours a Sunday given to God will not pay for a Monday devoted to the devil Mammon wore than to the devil Belial.

" Therefore, their lives are to be brought into the church. That is just what the church is for, that men should bring their lives into it, and measure them by the cubit of the sanctuary. They are there to be

32

reminded of the market, and the shop, and the ledger, and if the reminding stings them and pains them, so much the more do they need it. They are there to have their doings over the counter, on 'Change, in the street, in the forum, brought to the test of God's eternal law, that they may be saved from ruin. And the offertory is there to do this. That is the special use and need of that religious service in all times.

"The result, of course, if ever Christian men shall even begin to do their duty of giving on Christian principles, will be the world's conversion in about an ordinary lifetime. Meanwhile, let us begin to put this business of giving on its true ground. Let us deliver it from meanness and beggary, and teach what it is, a profound and solemn act of reverent worship and awe, before God's altar; an act wherein all mysteries meet in this, the deepest mystery of devotion that mortal man can give to the Eternal Lord and have the gift accepted."

To correct this spirit of disrespect now shown this legitimate and indispensable portion of worship, it will be necessary first to speak with becoming reverence of the offertory. Second, make the gathering of the offerings a part of the service, and let the people feel that it is a part of the worship. In accomplishing this let the pastor receive the offerings at the hands of the collectors, and then before turning from the congregation offer a brief consecrating prayer, asking God to accept the offerings and bless the givers. This brief prayer will do much to redeem the offertory and greatly stimulate and sweeten this act of worship and service.

The gathering of the offerings may also be solemnized and restored to its proper sacredness in the following manner: At the appropriate time let the minister arise and say, "the offerings of the people for benevolent purposes will now be gathered." While the collection is being taken, let the pastor slowly but distinctly pronounce the following or other appropriate passages of Scripture:

I. For Benevolent Purposes.

Trust in the Lord, and do good: so shalt thou dwell in the land, and verily thou shalt be fed.

Give, and it shall be given unto you; good measure, pressed down, and shaken together, and running over: for with the same measure that ye mete, it shall be measured to you again.

Take heed, and beware of covetousness: for a man's life consisteth not in the abundance of the things which he possesseth—but rather seek ye the kingdom of God, and all these things shall be added unto you.

There is that scattereth, and yet increaseth; and there is that withholdeth more than is meet, but it tendeth to poverty.

Honor the Lord with thy substance, and with the first-fruits of all thine increase: so shall thy barns be filled with plenty, and thy presses shall burst out with new wine.

The liberal deviseth liberal things ; and by libe-ral things shall he stand.

Charge them that are rich in this world—that they do good—that they be rich in good works, ready to distribute, willing to communicate ; laying up in store for themselves a good foundation against the time to come, that they may lay hold on eternal life.

Lay not up for yourselves treasures upon earth, where moth and rust doth corrupt, and where thieves break through and steal : but lay up for yourselves treasures in heaven, where neither moth nor rust doth corrupt, and where thieves do not break through nor steal : for where your treasure is, there will your heart be also.

But this I say, He which soweth sparingly shall reap also sparingly ; and he which soweth bountifully shall reap also bountifully. Every man according as he purposeth in his heart, so let him give ; not grudg-ingly, or of necessity ; for God loveth a cheerful giver.

II. Alms-Giving.

Blessed is he that considereth the poor. The Lord will deliver him in time of trouble. The Lord will preserve him, and keep him alive ; and he shall be blessed upon the earth ; and thou wilt not deliver him unto the will of his enemies. The Lord will strengthen him upon the bed of languishing : thou wilt make all his bed in his sickness.

Sell whatsoever thou hast, and give to the poor, and thou shalt have treasure in heaven.

Thou shalt not harden thy heart, nor shut thy hand from thy poor brother ; but thou shalt open thy hand wide unto him, and shalt surely lend him sufficient for his need, in that which he wanteth : thou shalt surely give him, and thy heart shall not be grieved when thou givest unto him ; because that for this thing, the Lord thy God shall bless thee in all thy works, and in all that thou puttest thy hand unto.

He that hath pity upon the poor lendeth unto the

Lord, and that which he hath given will he pay him again.

He that giveth unto the poor shall not lack.

Verily I say unto you, inasmuch as ye have done it unto one of the least of these, my brethren, ye have done it unto me.

And let us not be weary in well-doing; for in due season we shall reap, if we faint not.

CHAPTER VIII.

THE TITHE, FREE-WILL OFFERING AND ALMS-GIVING.

THE TITHE A PERPETUAL MEMORIAL OF GOD'S SOVEREIGNTY—IT WAS REQUIRED FROM THE BEGINNING—IT IS UNIVERSAL AND PERPETUAL — TITHES UNDER THE CLEARER LIGHT OF THE JEWISH DISPENSATION—VARIOUS TITHES AND OFFERINGS—THE TITHE IN THE NEW TESTAMENT CHURCH—HOW THE CHURCH CAME TO DEPART FROM THE LAW OF THE TITHE—WHAT ARE FREE-WILL OFFERINGS—WHAT ARE ALMS.

" The earth is the Lord's, and the fullness thereof; the world and they that dwell therein," and as everything belongs to God, it is reasonable that in God's first covenant with his creature, man, we should expect to find some requirement looking to the recognition of the relation of man as the subject, and of God as the Great Proprietor of all things. God did not cede his rights as proprietor to Adam, but he put him " into the garden of Eden to dress it and to keep it." Adam did not become the proprietor, but was God's tenant. The grant of every tree of the garden was a grant of the sole and only Proprietor, ceding limited privileges to man, the dependent subject of his

continual bounty and blessing. The one tree which
was reserved was to be a continual memorial of God's
ownership of the entire garden. Adam could not
have been tried, or proven, by the principles subsequently incorporated in the second table of the Law.
He had no father and mother to disobey, no being to
kill, or with whom to commit adultery, or from whom
to steal, or against whom to bear false witness, or the
possession of whose property he might covet. But he
was tested upon the principle which now lies at the
very foundation of the first and each succeeding command of the Decalogue. He was tested upon the
question of yielding implicit obedience to God as his
supreme sovereign.

Not only was God the Proprietor of Eden and its
products, which Adam was permitted to enjoy, but
even the breath which he breathed, the time—the
duration of his existence—this also, as well as everything, belonged to God. God was emphatically the
universal Sovereign ; as the universal Sovereign, "the
Lord God COMMANDED the man " concerning the
restrictions and limitations of his covenant, making
even the language of the command an explicit asser-
tion of sovereignty. He reserved one tree of the garden as a symbol of his sovereign ownership of all
the garden, and one day of each week, that day which
had been " sanctified," he reserved as a memorial of

his sovereign right to all of man's time. The angels coveted the glory which Christ had with the Father, and they fell; Adam and Eve coveted what belonged to God in Eden, and they fell; Judas coveted the wealth of the wicked, and he fell; Ananias and Sapphira coveted what they had voluntarily promised to give to Christ and his cause, and they fell—and so on from the beginning to the end of time, through the long catalogue of the succeeding generations, the sin of covetousness has been the besetting sin of mankind, and has called down the displeasure and punishment of heaven. It was to counteract this tendency of our natures, to avert the fearful consequences of this sin, that God *from the very first* required a continual and adequate acknowledgment of our dependency and his supremacy. God's relation to all created things is now and ever has been the same, man's nature is the same, and his well-being requires the same discipline and the same lessons of God's supremacy and man's dependency.

This brings us to the statement of our position in relation to the law of the tithe, which is, that this law was recognized from the beginning—it was not given for any limited time—it was not limited to any particular people—but that its binding force was recognized *from the beginning*, and sweeps on to the *end of time*, grasping in its divine requirements all ages, all nations, and all conditions of men alike.   33

From what has been said, it is undeniable that God's ownership is perpetual, inextinguishable, and under all circumstances indisputable and supreme. It has also been shown that God did, by explicit command in his first covenant with man, require some just and continual recognition of the fact that man was the mere tenant, and that God was the Great Proprietor of all things.

It cannot be denied that during the first two thousand five hundred years of the world's history man received no *written* revelation of the divine will. Until Moses received at the hand of God the commandments written with God's own finger upon tables of stone—until then the world had been governed by God's revealed but unrecorded will. Just the same as among the nations there are unwritten laws which together are called the Common Law. They embody the simplest, the most just, the most manifestly reasonable principles which lie at the foundation of all law. They grow out of the relations of men and the constituted nature of things, and are only written in our very being. There is also the written law, the Statute Law, expressed with all the requisite forms of legislation. Just so God has dealt with the human race. On mount Sinai the unwritten law was not abrogated, but received its confirmation by being expressed in the statutory laws of God.

The account given us in Genesis is an inspired account of the creation, and a history of the world for two thousand five hundred years. It is not a statutory book of laws, but a brief history of a long period. We cannot, therefore, expect to find in it a full record of all of God's requirements.

After man's expulsion from Eden, in the renewed covenant we find no permission to worship the God whom they had offended ; no instructions how to approach him with acceptable sacrifices, and yet this permission and instruction must most assuredly have been given them. After the flood, although Noah and his family had witnessed the injustice and the wicked practices of those before the flood, yet we find in the account of this renewed covenant no record of any requirements of duty to God, or of duty to his neighbor (except that concerning murder), nor of the observance of the Sabbath or of sacrifice, and yet we would not for a moment suppose that these were not enjoined.

Just so with regard to the then unwritten law of the tithe, while it was unwritten, yet it was most clearly observed.

Before the giving of the statutory law by the hand of Moses, there were various offerings of material things made to God, accounts of which, in a somewhat incidental manner, are recorded in the Bible :

" And in process of time it came to pass that Cain brought of the fruit of the ground an offering unto the Lord. And Abel, he also brought of the firstlings of his flock and of the fat thereof."—(Gen. iv. 3, 4).

" And Noah builded an altar unto the Lord; and took of every clean beast, and of every clean fowl, and offered burnt offerings on the altar."—(Gen. viii. 20).

" And the Lord appeared unto Abram, and said, Unto thy seed will I give this land : and there builded he an altar unto the Lord, who appeared unto him."—(Gen. xii. 7; see also, ver. 8; .xiii. 18; xxvi. 25; xxxiii. 20; xxxi. 1; xlvi. 1).

" And Melchizedek, King of Salem, brought forth bread and wine : and he was the priest of the most high God. And he blessed him, and said, Blessed be Abram of the most high God, possessor of heaven and earth : and blessed be the most high God, which hath delivered thine enemies into thy hand. And he gave him tithes of all."—(Gen. xiv. 18, 20; see also, xv. 9, 10).

" And Jacob rose up early in the morning, and took the stone that he had put for his pillows, and set it up for a pillar, and poured oil upon the top of it. And he called the name of that place Beth-el : but the name of that city was called Luz at the first. And Jacob vowed a vow, saying, if God will be with me, and will keep me in this way that I go, and will give

me bread to eat, and raiment to put on, so that I come again to my father's house in peace : then shall the Lord be my God : and this stone, which I have set for a pillar, shall be God's house: and of all that thou shalt give me I will surely give the tenth unto thee."
—(Gen. xxviii. 18, 22 ; see also, Ex. v. 1, 3 ; x. 25, 26 ; xii. 3, 26, 27 ; xviii. 12 ﹆

These passages of Scripture show :

1. That from the very first men offered to God of the choicest of beasts, fowls and cultivated fruits of the earth.

2. In the fact that Abel " brought of the firstlings of his flock " we see clearly that God had enjoined upon the family of Adam the duty of offering *the first* of that which the bountiful Giver bestowed upon them. The institution must necessarily have preceded the first mention of its observance, and since Abel's offering is declared to be an offering of " faith," it must have been in conformity to the divine command, else it could not have been offered " by faith."

3. That in two instances at least the tithe is explic- itly mentioned, and mentioned in a manner which indicates that Abram, in giving tithes to Melchizedek, simply conformed to an already established custom, and that Jacob at Beth-el simply vowed conformity to a law previously enjoined.

4. The tenth is the *least* amount which is either expressed or implied.

If we come to the law as recorded by Moses, we get a clearer understanding of the divine law of the tithe. As with the law of the Sabbath, the sacrifice and other laws, so with that of the tithe—it was authoritative from the beginning, it was known to the servants of God, and more or less obeyed by them. This re-enactment, or recording of the law was an endorsement whereby this law which had been universal became a re-enjoined law to the children of Israel. By its re-enactment God was emphasizing the importance of its continued observance. Here, then, we come to a more full and more clear understanding of the divine requirements respecting our relations and duty to him as the undisputed Sovereign of all things.

The law of the tithe, as we find it in the code of Israel's laws, consisted in this :

I—THE FIRST TITHE.

" And all the tithes of the land, whether of the seed of the land, or of the fruit of the tree, is the Lord's : it is holy unto the Lord. And if a man will at all redeem aught of his tithes, he shall add thereto the fifth part thereof. And concerning the tithe of the herd, or of the flock, even of whatsoever passeth under the rod, the tenth shall be holy unto the Lord. He shall not search whether it be good or bad, neither shall he change it : and if he change it at all, then both it and the change thereof shall be holy ; it shall not be redeemed."—(Lev. xxvii. 30, 33).

This one-tenth of the increase is that which was required from the beginning as *the least* that would meet the requirements of God's law. This was what still is emphatically *the Lord's tenth*, and by him it was wholly assigned to the support of his servants.

II—THE SECOND TITHE.

" Thou shalt truly tithe all the increase of thy seed, that the field bringeth forth year by year. And thou shalt eat before the Lord thy God, in the place which he shall choose to place his name there, the tithe of thy corn, of thy wine, and of thine oil, and the firstlings of thy herds and of thy flocks ; that thou mayest learn to fear the Lord thy God always. And if the way be too long for thee, so that thou art not able to carry it ; or if the place be too far from thee, which the Lord thy God shall choose to set his name there, when the Lord thy God hath blessed thee ; then shalt thou turn it into money, and bind up the money in thine hand, and shalt go unto the place which the Lord thy God shall choose: and thou shalt bestow that money for whatsoever thy soul lusteth after, for oxen, or for sheep, or for wine, or for strong drink, or for whatsoever thy soul desireth : and thou shalt eat there before the Lord thy God, and thou shalt rejoice, thou and thine household, and the Levite that is within thy gates ; thou shalt not forsake him : for he hath no part nor inheritance with thee."—(Deu. xiv. 22, 27).

This is a second tenth part of all the increase. This is not called the Lord's tithe, nor was it devoted to the maintenance of the Levites and priests, but was to be consumed by the family, together with some poorer brethren and some of the Levites, in feasting before the Lord in the place where he should appoint his worship to be offered.

III—THE THIRD TITHE.

" At the end of three years thou shalt bring forth all the tithe of thine increase the same year, and shalt lay it up within thy gates : and the Levite, because he hath no part nor inheritance with thee, and the stranger, and the fatherless, and the widow, which are within thy gates, shall come, and shall eat and be satisfied ; that the Lord thy God may bless thee in all the work of thine hand which thou doest."—(Deu. xiv. 28, 29; see also, xxvi. 12, 13).

This appears to be a third tenth of all increase, which was required only every third year, and was devoted at home to the entertainment of the Levites, strangers, fatherless and widows residing in each one's more immediate neighborhood. That it was to be consumed at home, seems to mark it as a tithing distinct and separate from the other two, yet it is but fair to state that by some this is regarded as identical with the second tithing, being distinguished only in this, that upon each third year it was diverted from its general use to a special or particular purpose.

IV—THE FOURTH TITHE.

" Thus speak unto the Levites, and say unto them. When ye take of the children of Israel the tithes which I have given you from them for your inherit-ance, then ye shall offer up a heave offering of it for the Lord, even a tenth part of the tithe. Thus ye also shall offer a heave offering unto the Lord of all your tithes, which ye receive of the children of Israel ; and ye shall give thereof the Lord's heave offering to Aaron the priest."—(Num. xviii. 26, 28).

This fourth tithe was that which the Lord required the Levites to pay to the priests. The Levites were those who were descended from Levi by Gershom, Kohath and Merari, and were called Levites as dis-tinguished from the sons of Levi by Aaron, who were called the priests.

Beside these tithes, there were the various forms of sacrifices and offerings comprising the burnt-offering, the meat-offering, the peace-offering, the sin-offering, and the trespass-offering.* In addition to these, there

---

*The regular sacrifices in the temple service were : I. Burnt-of-ferings : (a.) The daily burnt-offerings (Ex. xxix. 38, 42). (b.) The double burnt-offerings on the Sabbath (Num. xxviii. 9, 10). (c.) The burnt-offerings at the great festivals (Num. xxviii. 11 ; xxix. 39). II. Meat-offerings : (a.) The daily meat-offerings accompanying the daily burnt-offerings (flour, wine, oil), (Ex. xxix. 40, 41). (b.) The shew-bread (Lev. xxiv. 5, 9). (c.) Spe-cial meat-offerings at the Sabbath and the great festivals (Num. xxviii., xxix.). (d.) The first-fruits at the Passover (Lev. xxiii.

were 'the numerous provisions for the poor, besides the offerings of the people for themselves as individuals at the purification of women (Lev. xii.', the presentation of the first-born at circumcision, the cleansing of the leprosy (Lev. xiv.', of the unclean (Lev. xv.', at the fulfillment of vows (Num. vi. 1, 20, at marriages and funerals, etc., etc., besides the frequent offering of private sin-offerings. To meet the various requirements must have demanded from one-fourth to one-third of all the annual production of the entire land.

The law of the tithe and of the offering which were held by worshipers from the first, and which had become world-wide before the time of Moses, were multiplied and intensified under the Jewish dispensation. As more was given, so more was required.

THE TITHE IN THE NEW TESTAMENT CHURCH.

On this subject of the tithe the Old and New Tes-

10, 14); at Pentecost (Lev. xxiii. 17, 20), both called wave-offerings; the first-fruits of the dough and threshing-floor at harvest (Num. xv. 20, 21; Deut. xxvi. 1, 11), called heave offerings. III. Sin-offerings: (*a.*) A kid each new moon (Num. xxviii. 15). (*b.*) Sin-offerings at the Passover, Pentecost, Feast of Trumpets and Tabernacles (Num. xxviii. 22, 30; xxix. 5, 16, 19, 22, 25, 28, 31, 34, 38). (*c.*) The offering of the two goats (one sacrificed and the other the scape goat) for the people, and the bullock for the priest himself, on the Great Day of Atonement (Lev. xvi.). IV. Incense: (*a.*) The morning and evening incense (Ex. xxx. 7, 8). (*b.*) The incense on the Great Day of Atonement (Lev. xvi. 12).

taments are not to be arrayed as though their declarations were at variance upon this great doctrine. They are an exposition not of two, but of one system of religion—the Christian religion. The same divine principles and moral laws pervade both dispensations alike, and the same lessons are taught in both. It was of the Old Testament that Christ said : " Search the Scriptures ; for in them ye think ye have eternal life, and they are they which testify of me." These were the " Holy Scriptures " which Timothy had known " from a child," which were " profitable for doctrine, for reproof, for correction, for instruction in righteousness." " They are not two churches," says Leslie, "but two states of the same church ; for it is the same Christian church from the first promise of Christ (Gen iii. 15) to the end of the world, and therefore it is said (Heb. iv. 2) that the gospel was preached unto them as well as unto us." The civil and ceremonial laws, given to a particular people for a particular time, became null and void when that time was accomplished ; but the law of the tithe existed from the first, and was neither civil nor ceremonial, but moral, and consequently it is just as binding to-day as any other unchangable moral law.

Since the church is the same, and governed by the same laws under both dispensations, these laws were not reannounced by Christ ; they were taken for granted, they were understood, they were recognized, for Jesus declared concerning the law and the prophets that " he came not to destroy, but to fulfil." This was his endorsement, and they needed not to be reannounced. The law of the tithe needed not to be announced any more than the law of the Sabbath, or of prayer, or worship. Jesus sanctioned the great liberality of Zaccheus when he gave " half his goods," and even when a poor widow gave " all her living," the act secured his fullest commendation, and to the young man who came running to him Jesus made the parting with *all* his " great possessions " the condition upon which rested his salvation. The first worship to the infant Saviour was in the richest treasures of " gold, frankincense and myrrh," and so must all true worship of him ever be attended. When the Pharisees boasted of giving tithes of " mint and anise and cummin," Christ reproved them for omitting " judgment, mercy, faith," but approved of their paying tithes even to the utmost.

There was no occasion for a continual repetition of this law to the apostles and early Christians. When this abiding truth was baptized by the Pentecostal blessing, we find them selling their possessions and goods, and parting them to all men as every man had need—thus again and again we find them even out of

a deep poverty abounding in the riches of their liberality, being " willing of themselves."*

That the law of the tithe was recognized, and the
duty of conformity to it enforced, is made very evident in the writings of the Fathers, and in the records
of the councils of the church.†

Since the tithe was instituted soon after the creation of man, was observed before the giving of the
Law on mount Sinai, was emphasized and intensified

---

*See also, Acts ii. 44, 45 ; iv. 34, 35 ; ix. 36, 39 ; xvi. 15, 33,
34 ; xx. 35 ; xxviii. 14, 15 ; Rom, xv. 25. 28 ; xvi. 1, 2, 6 ; I Cor.
xvi, 1, 2, 15 ; II Cor. viii. 1, 4 ; ix. 1, 2, 12, 15 ; Phil. iv. 10, 14,
16: I Thess. iv. 9, 10.

†As our space and purpose in this treatise are too limited to
admit of the presentation of the quotations which establish this
point, we refer the reader to the following works of the Fathers :
Irenæus. Adversus Hæresus, Lib. 4. Cap. 27, 34 ; Origen, In
Numero Homilia xi., In Genes. Hom. xvi ; Cyprian, De Unit.
Eccles. § 23 ; Chrysostom, Tom. i., Hom. 35, Tom. ii., Ad Eph.
Hom. iv., Ad I Cor. Hom. 43, Ad Act. Hom. 18 ; Ambrose, Ad
Hom. 33 et 34 ; Jerome. Epist. 2, Ad Nepotianum, In Malachiam
iii., In Epis. 1 Cor. In Ezek. xliv. ; Augustine, De Reddendis Dec-
imis, Ser. 219, In Psalmum cxlvi., Hom. 48 ; see also, Council of
Ancyra (A. D. 314) ; of Gangra (A. D. 324) ; of Orleans (first),
(A. D. 511) ; of Mascon (second Council), (A. D. 585) ; of Se-
ville (first Council). (A. D. 590) ; of Toledo (fourth), (A. D. 633);
of Friuli (A. D. 791). Besides these, many subsequent Councils.
In the confessional at this period was asked : " Hast thou at any
time neglected to pay thy tithes to God, which God himself
ordained to be given ? If thou hast done so, or consented to the
defrauding of the church therein, first restore to God fourfold the
tenth of all kinds of possessions, as well personal as prædial."

under the Mosaic dispensation, was recognized by Christ, and the Christian church was built around it, and since it was recognized by the Christian church in the earlier centuries, how does it come that in these later centuries the Christian church has departed from this law?

About three centuries before the Reformation the apostate church of Rome assailed the doctrine of the *Divine Right of the Tithe.* She taught that tithes not being of divine right, might be alienated from the support of the priests to the aggrandizement of the church. To justify corrupt practices it was necessary to supplant divine laws by corrupt doctrines. This the Man of Sin did not hesitate to do, but substituted the doctrine of *Competent Maintenance* for the divine law of the tithe. The State was not slow to learn the lesson. If tithes did not belong to God, and God's ministers were entitled only to a " competent mainten- ance," why was not the State as justly entitled to the tithes of the people as the Pope? and why could not the State appropriate the tithes and dole out to the clergy a " competent maintenance " as well as the Pope ?*   Thus, in the sixteenth century, we have the

---

*God appropriated the tithes of the people for the maintenance of the Levites; they were not to be used for the support of the State. Under the Mosaic dispensation the Crown was to be sup- ported by presents (I Saml. x. 27); by the products of the royal

State under the protection of this corrupt doctrine, wresting from the church those tithes which God had devoted to her support. As every student of history knows, the effects were as disastrous as the doctrine was delusive. Here we have, then, briefly, how these tithes, which " *are the* Lord's," were in the first diverted from the purposes to which God had devoted them, and how they were finally entirely alienatd from the Church by the State. The history from that time to this is only too well known to need recording here —a Church dependent upon the State, or dependent upon the merest pittance of the people. From that time to this the history of the church has been one of servile dependence either upon the State or upon the people. At the remembrance of the sad results of the past, and the degrading slavery of the present, we can but sit down as Israel " by the rivers of Babylon," and " weep when we remember Zion."

---

flocks (I Saml. xxi. 7, 8; II Chron, xxxii. 28, 29); by the royal demesnes, vineyards and olive gardens (I Chron. xxvii. 26, 28); by the spoils of conquered nations (I Kings iv. 21; II Chron. xxvii. 5); by the tribute of conquered nations and of merchants passing through their country [I Kings x. 15]; by taxes and tolls [Ezra iv. 14, 19, 20]; by a tenth, which Samuel forewarned them that the king, like the kings of other nations, would exact [I Saml. viii. 15]. That the treasuries of the Lord's house and of the king's house were distinct, see II Kings xviii. 15, and II Chron. xii. 9.

II—FREE-WILL OFFERINGS.

To arrive at a clear understanding of the difference between tithes, offerings, and free-will offerings, it will be necessary to state them connectedly. The tithe is the one-tenth (as the name indicates) of a man's yearly increase, or income, which God has reserved, and appointed to be returned to him. The tithe is " holy unto the Lord," and in rendering the tithe man gives nothing of his own to God, but simply returns to God that which was always his, and which he only entrusts into the hands of man as his steward, and by which to attest his honesty and remind him that God is the supreme Sovereign even of the nine-tenths which he is permitted to retain. The term tithe, then, comprehends the first one-tenth of the yearly increase of the people, which God requires the people to return to him, and which, under the Mosaic dispensation, was assigned by him for the maintenance of the Levites. It also comprehends the one-tenth which the Levites were to give of all the tithes they received from the people, and which is called a heave-offering, which the Lord assigned for the maintenance of the Priests. Technically, the term " tithe " does •not include the second tenth of the annual increase which was devoted to a sacred feasting before the Lord in the place which he should appoint ; nor does it include the third tithe used every third year for a local feasting of the Levite, the stranger, the fatherless and the widow—these tithes are classed among offerings. Strictly or technically, then, the term tithe refers only to that first tithe of the people and the heave-offering of the Levites, which was holy unto the Lord.

The term *offerings*, in its more comprehensive sense, includes all that man gives in any shape to God as an expression of love and obedience, or for the service of his fellow-man, *after* having rendered to God the one-tenth of all his increase. Between tithes and offerings, there exists a difference as to property. In sacrifices and offerings man gives of his own to God ; he gives to God that which he might withhold, and not defraud God of that, the right of which he has never ceded to man. By withholding his offerings, man dishonors God ; by withholding the tithes, he defrauds God of that which is, and always was his, and which was never man's at all. In offerings man is permitted, in a large measure, to exercise his reason and to gratify his wishes, but in the payment of the tithe, God both appoints the measure and designates the use.

While the term *offering* includes the *free-will* offering, it comprehends much more. The free-will offerings of the people were those gifts which were contributed for the erecting or the repairing of the tabernacle, temple or any place made sacred to the worship

35

of Jehovah, or to provide outward things necessary for the service of God's house.*

The free-will offering is *obligatory* in character, although unprescribed in amount, which is left to each one's conscience and love to God—hence they are called free-will offerings. " Every man shall give as he is able, according to the blessing of the Lord thy God which he hath given thee."—(Deu. xvi. 17.)

ALMS-GIVING.

God has designed that in every age and nation and clime there shall be living illustrations of the condition of dependence and want to which Christ condescended for our salvation. " The poor shall never cease out of the land," saith the Lord. The way in which they are *ever* to be treated is clearly manifest in the Mosaic dispensation. The grain was not to be reaped from the corners of the fields, but was to be left for the poor, the gleanings of the fields and of the vineyards belonged to them. The poor were to participate in the second tithe, or festival tithe, and every third year a special tithe was levied for their especial benefit. The products of the Sabbatical year were theirs, besides the cancelling of their debts, the restoration of their freedom, and returning

*See Ex. xxv. 1, 2, 3; Lev. xxii. 18, 19, 24; xxiii. 38; Ezra i. 4; iii. 5; viii. 28; II Chron. xxxi. 14. See also, "The Scriptural Plan," Chapter V., page 175.

of their estates upon the return of every year of Jubilee. The Old Testament abounds with instruction concerning our treatment of the poor: "If there be among you a poor man of one of thy brethren within any of thy gates in thy land which the Lord thy God giveth·thee, thou shalt not harden thine heart, nor shut thine hand from thy poor brother: but thou shalt open thine hand wide unto him, and shalt surely lend him sufficient for his need, in that which he wanteth. Beware that there be not a thought in thy wicked heart, saying, The seventh year, the year of release, is at hand ; and thine eye be evil against thy poor brother, and thou givest him nought; and he cry unto the Lord against thee, and it be sin unto thee. Thou shalt surely give him, and thine heart shall not be grieved when thou givest unto him : because that for this thing the Lord thy God shall bless thee in all thy works, and in all that thou puttest thine hand unto. For the poor shall never cease out of the land : therefore I command thee, saying, Thou shalt open thine hand wide unto thy brother, to thy poor, and to thy needy, in thy land."—(Deut. xv. 7–11).*

" It was the practice of the Lord Jesus to direct funds from their treasury, from time to time, to be given to the poor. So common a thing was it to make

*See also, Lev. xxiii. 22; xix. 10; Ex. xxiii. 11; Deut. xv. 1, 2, 12; Ex. xxi. 2.

such drafts on the treasury, that when Jesus at the table told Judas, ' What thou doest, do quickly,' the other disciples thought he meant that a donation should be made to the poor."

The early Christians so excelled in their acts of charity that this remarkable feature of their religion excited the wonder of the heathen world. " But whoso hath this world's good, and seeth his brother have need, and shutteth up his bowels of compassion from him, how dwelleth the love of God in him?"— (I John iii. 17).

The same duty still exists, and if the Christian church had not so far forgotten her duty in this matter of caring for the poor, there would now be no score of societies organized outside of the church for the purpose of doing the church's work.

But we have introduced this section to show by contrast what alms-giving is in the light of God's Word, and also to show that this is a special and distinct portion of Christian duty. That portion of our goods which we give to the poor is not to take the place of our offerings to the Lord. Neither are our alms to be drawn from that portion of God's bounty which is " holy unto the Lord." " If we give to the poor out of God's tenth, we give what is none of our own ; we rob God to pay man, and commit a sacrilege for the sake of charity."

CONCLUSION.

That tithes, offerings and alms are still expected of Christian people there can not exist the least doubt in any well-informed mind. But how have we discharged the obligation? Have we been faithful stewards, and are we ready to render an account of our stewardship? No; many have not heeded, most have not even known their duty, and all have come short of both privilege and obligation. God has not deprived us of the blessedness of giving. The same unchanged command guards the limits of THE LEAST, while the promises and offered blessings of the New Testament invite the worshiper to offer more under the Christian than under the Mosaic dispensation. The same impending judgments are still attendant upon the violation of these laws. In the days of Haggai, at the close of Judah's long captivity, when the people came back to their desolated land, their thought was not of worship, of sacrifice, of tithes and of offerings, but of the rebuilding of their own houses and the enriching of themselves while they neglected their duty to God and to his house, God said: " Consider your ways. Ye have sown much, and bring in little; ye eat, but ye have not enough; ye drink, but ye are not filled with drink; ye clothe you, but there is none warm; and he that earneth wages, earneth wages to put it into a bag with holes. Ye looked for much, and, lo, it came to little; and when ye brought it home, I did blow upon it. Why? saith the Lord of hosts. Because of mine house that is waste, and ye run every man unto his own house. Therefore the heaven over you is stayed from dew, and the earth is stayed from her fruit. —(Haggai i. 6, 9, 10.)

Are not these same sad consequences being realized to-day in the spiritual history of the church? Look at the thousands of churches all over this broad land, struggling with debts, treasuries empty, people disheartened, current expenses not met, the great work of the church impeded, the poor and destitute neglected, the heathen left to die in darkness, the servants of God in a state of humiliating dependence—not a few struggling with debts, many in want, and some in positive mental and physical distress. The picture is not overdrawn, nor the facts overstated. As God's husbandmen, we " sow much, and bring in little," the church " drinks, but is not filled, is clothed, but is not warm, it gathers, but it puts it into a bag with holes."

Have we not an answer to the cause of all this? It is the same now as when Malachi reproved the priests in his day, saying : " Ye are departed out of the way ; ye have caused many to stumble at the law ; ye have corrupted the covenant of Levi, saith the Lord of hosts. Therefore, have I also made you contemptible and base before all the people, according as ye have not kept my ways, *but have been partial in the law.* Have we not all one father? hath not one God created us? why do we deal treacherously every man against his brother, by profaning the covenant of our fathers? Even from the days of your fathers ye are gone away from mine ordinances, and have not kept them. Return unto me, and I will return unto you, saith the Lord of hosts. But ye said, Wherein shall we return? Will a man rob God? Yet ye have robbed me. But ye say, Wherein have we robbed thee? IN TITHES AND OFFERINGS. Ye are cursed with a curse; for ye have robbed me even this whole nation. Bring ye all the tithes into the storehouse, that there may be meat in mine house, [*i. e.* support for my ministers and my service] and prove me now herewith, saith the Lord of hosts, if I will not open you the windows of heaven, and pour you out a blessing, that there shall not be room enough to receive it. And I will rebuke the devourer for your sakes, and he shall not destroy the fruits of your ground; neither shall your vine cast her fruit before the time in the field, saith the Lord of hosts. And all nations shall call you blessed! for ye shall be a delightsome land, saith the Lord of hosts."—(Mal. ii. 8-10; iii. 7-12.)

THE END.

KNAPP & FINCH, PRINTERS, EASTON, PA.

www.ingramcontent.com/pod-product-compliance
Lightning Source LLC
Chambersburg PA
CBHW030630030726
47497CB00006B/1724